LET'S STUDY
1 & 2 THESSALONIANS

Let's Study

1 & 2 THESSALONIANS

Andrew W. Young

THE BANNER OF TRUTH TRUST

THE BANNER OF TRUTH TRUST
3 Murrayfield Road, Edinburgh EH12 6EL, UK
P.O. Box 621, Carlisle, PA 17013, USA

❋

© Andrew W. Young 2001
First Published 2001
ISBN 0 85151 798 6

❋

Typeset in 11/12pt Ehrhardt MT at the
Banner of Truth Trust, Edinburgh

Printed in Great Britain by
Bell & Bain Ltd.,
Glasgow

To the memory of

WILLEM VAN RIJ (1913–1998)

MENTOR AND FRIEND

Contents

Publisher's Preface

Let's Study 1 and 2 Thessalonians is part of a series of books which explain and apply the message of Scripture. The series is designed to meet a specific and important need in the church. While not technical commentaries, each volume will comment on the text of a biblical book; and while not merely lists of practical applications, they are concerned with the ways in which the teaching of Scripture can affect and transform our lives today. Understanding the Bible's message and applying its teaching are the aims.

Like other volumes in the series, *Let's Study 1 and 2 Thessalonians* seeks to combine explanation and application. Its concern is to be helpful to ordinary Christian people by encouraging them to understand the message of the Bible and apply it to their own lives. The reader in view is not the person who is interested in all the detailed questions which fascinate the scholar, although behind the writing of each study lies an appreciation for careful and detailed scholarship. The aim is exposition of Scripture written in the language of a friend, seated alongside you with an open Bible.

Let's Study 1 and 2 Thessalonians is designed to be used in various contexts. It can be used simply as an aid for individual Bible study. Some may find it helpful to use in their devotions with husband or wife, or to read in the context of the whole family.

In order to make these studies more useful, not only for individual use but also for group study in Sunday School classes and home, church or college, study guide material will be found on pp. 175–193. Sometimes we come away frustrated rather than helped by group discussions. Frequently that is because we have been encouraged to discuss a passage of Scripture which we do not understand very well in the first place. Understanding must always be the foundation for enriching discussion and for thoughtful, practical application. Thus, in addition to the exposition of 1 and 2 Thessalonians, the additional material provides questions to encourage personal thought and study, or to be used as discussion starters. The Group Study Guide divides the material into thirteen sections and provides direction for leading and participating in group study and discussion.

The text which forms the basis of the studies is *The New International Version.*

Paul and the Thessalonians

The Thessalonian letters are among the earliest of the Apostle Paul's letters found in the New Testament. In fact, with the exception perhaps of his letter to the Galatians and the epistle of James, they are possibly the very earliest of all our New Testament documents.

They were prompted by the intense concern that Paul and his co-workers Silas and Timothy felt for Christians in the city of Thessalonica (present-day Thessaloniki). The three men had been forced to abandon their mission in that city prematurely and knew they were leaving behind a vulnerable young church to face torrid opposition. They could not help but be concerned for those who had so recently become their brothers and sisters in Christ.

Little wonder, then, that upon learning of their condition some weeks (or perhaps months) later, Paul was spurred to write to them in a way that reflected his deep care for them. A tender pastoral note is perhaps the most distinctive feature of these two letters. Although not commonly called 'pastoral epistles', the Thessalonian letters are nevertheless thoroughly pastoral in character. A fuller grasp of the circumstances that lay behind them will help us appreciate them more deeply.

VISIT TO THESSALONICA

Paul and his missionary colleagues Silas and Timothy visited Thessalonica some time in the year A.D. 51 in the course of what is usually called Paul's second missionary journey. The apostle, accompanied by Silas, had left his home base in Syrian Antioch some months before, intending to revisit the churches he and Barnabas had established on an earlier missionary journey (*Acts* 16:40). In Lystra they added Timothy to their party (*Acts* 16:1–3), and through the leading of the Holy Spirit, eventually found themselves in the town of Troas in the far west of the Roman province of Asia (modern Turkey). There in a night vision they received a call to cross over into Macedonia, a summons they hastened to obey (*Acts* 16:6–10).

After arriving at the port of Neapolis, the three missionaries travelled northwest to the Roman colony of Philippi (*Acts* 16:11–12). Luke, who had apparently joined them in Troas (note the 'we' in Acts 16:10–11), was now with them. During the several days they stayed in Philippi, their preaching resulted in the birth of a church.

Paul, Silas and Timothy, however, soon found themselves having to make a hurried exit from the city after being shamefully treated by its officials (*Acts* 16:38–40; *1 Thess.* 2:2). Leaving Luke behind with the new converts, they set out in a general west-southwest direction on the Roman road known as the Egnatian Way. After a journey of about 150 kilometers, which took them through the important towns of Amphipolis and Apollonia, they eventually reached the seaport of Thessalonica, the capital and most influential town in Macedonia.

Cassander, one of Alexander the Great's important army officers, had founded the city of Thessalonica in 315 B.C. To do so he had taken the inhabitants of Thermes, a nearby village famous for its hot springs, and the people belonging to twenty-five other villages and used them to form the founding population of a new city. He named this city Thessalonica after his wife, the daughter of King Philip II and half-sister of Alexander. It quickly gained prominence in the region, and by the year 46 B.C. had become the capital of the province.

As a strategically placed seaport, the city became famous for trade and commerce. Jews were attracted to it, as they were to commercial centres throughout the world of that time. Their arrival added a new dimension to the religious life of the city. Its native inhabitants worshipped the Roman pantheon of gods (including the emperor himself), and a host of oriental deities.

In this environment, the Jews, with their strict monotheism and high ethical standards, formed a class apart. Many Gentiles found the new religion an attractive alternative and attached themselves loosely to the Jewish community, becoming known as 'God-fearers.'

They attended synagogue meetings and embraced many of the teachings and practices they encountered. However, the exclusive nationalism of the Jews and the ritual requirements of their religion restrained most onlookers from actually becoming proselytes.

It was this Jewish community and its adherents that the missionaries targeted when they arrived in the city (*Acts* 17:2). On the Sabbath day they made their way to the synagogue, where they found opportunity to tell their message. Taking the Old Testament Scriptures, Paul demonstrated that the promised Messiah – for whose coming all earnest Jews longed – was to suffer, die and rise again before entering his glory. He then rehearsed the events of the life of Jesus of Nazareth, proving that in his death and resurrection the promises of the prophets had been fulfilled (*Acts* 17:3). The Jesus of history, in other words, was the Messiah (or Christ) of Scripture.

For three Sabbath days Paul reasoned in this way with his synagogue audience. Some Jews believed in what he said and identified themselves with the missionaries. So, too, did a 'large number of God-fearing Greeks and not a few prominent women of the city' (*Acts* 17:4). In this way, a Christian church came into existence in Thessalonica.

Just how long the three missionaries continued to preach in the city is uncertain. It does seem, however, that they stayed there for some time. They were there long enough for Paul to find productive work to support himself and Silas and Timothy (*2 Thess.* 3:8), for the church at Philippi to send aid more than once (*Phil.* 4:16), and for a significant number of pagan Gentiles to become believers (*1 Thess.* 1:9). In all likelihood, the initial brief Jewish mission in the synagogue was followed by a longer Gentile mission in the market place.

DEPARTURE FROM THESSALONICA

As happened in most cities where they preached, the three missionaries soon encountered opposition. Jealous Jews were their first adversaries. Embittered by the mass defection of God-fearers to the apostle and his companions, they set about harassing the preachers. They did so by enlisting a mob of thugs to start a riot in the city (*Acts* 17:5). A frenzied crowd rushed to the home of Jason – the missionaries' host – where they tried to lay hands on Paul and Silas. Failing to find the two men there, they hustled Jason himself and some other believers before the city officials (called politarchs, the elected magistrates of a free city) and there laid charges against them and the missionaries.

Jason was accused of harbouring men who had been 'causing trouble all over the world' (*Acts* 17:6 'turning the world upside down', AV). Specifically, these men he was hosting were guilty of defying the emperor by saying that there was another king, namely, Jesus.

These were by no means slight accusations. They amounted to charges of sedition and treason. Little wonder, then, that the crowd and the city officials were thrown into turmoil. To protect traitors was not a safe thing for any city to do.

Jason and the men with him were forced to post bond before being let go (*Acts* 17:9). Presumably this means that they were charged in some way with maintaining the peace of the city. Given the inflammatory attitude of the Jews, this must have seemed impossible to do if Paul and his companions remained with them. On that account, the brothers decided that it was best for the missionaries to leave Thessalonica for a time at least. So when night came, they sent them on their way to Berea (*Acts* 17:10).

CONCERN FOR THESSALONICA

Leaving the new community of believers was by no means easy for Paul, Silas and Timothy. Writing to them some months later, they could speak of being 'torn away' from them (*1 Thess.* 3:1). Out of sight, the Thessalonian Christians were by no means out of mind.

More than once Paul tried to return to them, but for one reason or another he was unable to do so. Eventually, after having been forced to leave Berea, the apostle found a way of re-establishing contact from Athens. Choosing to be left alone there, he commissioned Timothy to go and visit the Thessalonian Christians (*1 Thess.* 3:1–2). He was to strengthen and encourage them in the faith, and to bring back a report of their spiritual welfare.

Paul had moved on to Corinth by the time Timothy returned from this mission (*Acts* 18:5). His report comforted and cheered the apostle. He was able to say that the Thessalonians were still holding true to the gospel, that they had made progress in faith, love and hope, that they still remembered Paul with deep affection, and that they longed to see him again. Joy and gratitude filled the apostle's heart to hear these things, prompting a new wave of earnest prayer for doors to open that he might revisit them himself (*1 Thess.* 3:10).

It would seem, however, that not everything Timothy told Paul about the church in Thessalonica caused elation. Apparently there were problems and needs as well. From the letter that Paul wrote soon afterwards (1 Thessalonians), it appears that the Jews had embarked on a smear campaign against the apostle. They were trying to undermine the gospel by slandering its preachers, claiming that they were just another of the many bands of self-seeking maverick philosophers that tramped the Egnatian Way.

But this was not all. Persecution had escalated as pagan compatriots of the new believers joined Jews in opposing them (*1 Thess.* 2:14). Within the church itself confusion about aspects of the Lord's return was causing anxiety on the part of some, and indolence on the part of others (*1 Thess.* 4:13–5:11). Tendencies to revert to the lesser moral standards of the pagan world (*1 Thess.* 4:3–8), tensions between leaders in the church and members in the congregation (5:12–13), and difficulties connected with the ministry and gifts of the Holy Spirit (5:19–20) may also have been present.

LETTERS TO THESSALONICA

News of these things stirred Paul to write the letter we know as 1 Thessalonians. Thrilled as he was with the progress the church had made, he was not one to let his converts bask in their achievements. More than that, news of their troubles always prompted him to offer instruction, encouragement and, where necessary, rebuke. The pastor's heart in Paul turned him into a letter writer. Through letters he could establish a personal presence with his scattered flock and in this way continue to shepherd and care for them. Later, upon hearing further news of the congregation, he would write a second letter (2 Thessalonians) to remedy the continuing defects and needs of the fledgling church.

Given the relationship between Paul and the Thessalonian Christians, it should not surprise us that his letters to them throb with tenderness and care. Unlike some of the epistles he was to write later to other churches, they are relatively free from rigorous argument and sharp warning. Their lack of extended doctrinal discussion has caused some to underrate them, but that judgment is unwarranted. The absence of substantial blocks of teaching does not mean that these letters are bereft of theology. As we shall see, Paul pastors his converts with the gospel. Either implicitly or explicitly he does in fact touch on most of the major themes found elsewhere in his writings. That they do not appear in bold light in the Thessalonian letters is no reflection of his theological maturity, or of the worth of the letters themselves. It rather reflects that Paul is writing an authentic letter to a particular group of people, addressing their specific needs in the most appropriate way.

With that in mind, we can approach these letters confident of being taught and enriched. Here we can gain a glimpse into the life of a young first-century church facing severe opposition. We will see its defects and its strengths. But more than that, we will see in Paul and his companions a model of pastoral care. Here, perhaps as nowhere else in his letters, we see how the apostle loved his converts and laboured to lead them on in the faith. This should make every serious Christian, and especially every responsible Christian leader, turn with eagerness to the text of the letters that await us.

The Thessalonian Letters at a Glance

1 THESSALONIANS

1. Introduction
   (i) Opening greetings (1:1)
   (ii) Thanksgiving for the Thessalonians (1:2–10)

2. Paul and the Thessalonians
   (i) The apostolic mission in Thessalonica (2:1–16)
   (ii) Continuing concern for the Thessalonians (2:17–3:13)

3. A call to holy living
   (i) The challenge to further progress (4:1–2)
   (ii) The issue of sexual purity (4:3–8)
   (iii) Progress in brotherly love (4:9–10)
   (iv) Fruitful daily living (4:11–12)

4. Concerns about the second coming
   (i) Believers who have died before Jesus comes (4:13–18)
   (ii) The timing of the day of the Lord (5:1–11)

5. Practical instructions for church life
   (i) Respecting leaders (5:12–13)
   (ii) Caring for one another (5:14–15)
   (iii) Worshipping together (5:16–22)

6. Conclusion
   (i) A prayer for sanctification (5:23–24)
   (ii) Closing requests (5:25–27)
   (iii) A final greeting (5:28)

1 Thessalonians

I

Making Connections

Paul, Silas and Timothy, To the church of the Thessalonians in God the Father and the Lord Jesus Christ: Grace and peace to you (1 Thess. 1:1).

Readers of the New Testament soon recognise a similarity in the way the Apostle Paul begins his letters. They all follow the same basic form. Paul starts by introducing himself and any associates he may include with him. Then he identifies his readers and follows this with a greeting. From that point his letters commonly (though not always) flow into a section in which he thanks God for his readers. This was the way that correspondents usually started their letters in his day.

Similar though the opening words of his letters may be, they are never – with the exception of the two Thessalonian letters – quite the same. Paul adapted his introductions to suit his purposes. They often reflect something of his relationship with his readers and sometimes offer hints of themes that will follow in the body of the letter. Each ends up with its own distinctive character and invites careful study.

THE WRITER AND HIS ASSOCIATES

The two Thessalonian letters begin with the words 'Paul, Silas and Timothy' – the three men who had been responsible for establishing a Christian congregation in Thessalonica. Paul was the senior of the trio in that he was an apostle of the Lord Jesus Christ. He had received a commission to take the gospel to the Gentiles (*Acts* 9:15; 26:16–18) and represented the authority of the Lord in a special sense. He had also initiated the missionary journey that had eventually taken the three men to Thessalonica (*Acts* 15:36).

Silas (or Silvanus) was originally a respected member and prophet of the church in Jerusalem. He had taken part in the meeting of elders and apostles in Jerusalem that had determined whether or not the Gentile Christians needed to observe Jewish customs (*Acts* 15). As a measure of his standing, he was chosen to accompany Paul and Barnabas back to Antioch to explain and confirm the decision of the meeting (*Acts* 15:32). Paul later asked him to be his travelling companion after a serious dispute ruptured relationships with his earlier fellow missionary, Barnabas.

Timothy was the junior member of the missionary team. The son of a Jewish mother and a Greek father, he had risen to a place of high esteem among the churches of Lystra and Iconium, churches established by Paul and Barnabas during an earlier missionary campaign (*Acts* 16:1ff.). In the course of revisiting these churches with Silas, Paul learned of Timothy and asked him to accompany them. Before doing so he was circumcised to prevent offending the Jews of that area. Timothy was to become Paul's most intimate and valued helper in the years ahead.

Given that the three men had together visited Thessalonica and were known and loved by the Christians there, it is natural that the Thessalonian letters should claim to come from all three. Yet the extent to which Silas and Timothy were actually involved in composing them is unclear. While for the most part both letters are written in the first person plural ('we', 'our' or 'us'), there are occasions when Paul is clearly the sole author (*1 Thess.* 2:18; 3:5; 5:27; *2 Thess.* 3:17). It may be that the three men consulted and prayed together about the contents of the letters before Paul dictated them, possibly to Silas. All three certainly shared the same concern for the Thessalonians, and undoubtedly all concurred with what was written. We will assume that Paul is the primary author and attribute both letters to him, understanding as we do that Silas and Timothy may have had some role in their composition.

The simplicity with which the three names are introduced is noteworthy. Most writers in the first century began their letters with their personal names but occasionally added a title as well to underline their authority or status. Paul usually does this in his letters. Commonly he describes himself as 'an apostle of Jesus Christ' or perhaps as 'a servant of Jesus Christ' (*e.g.*, *Rom.* 1:1). That he does not in the Thessalonian letters probably indicates that he felt no need to emphasise his authority to this group of believers. Relations between them were close and amicable. The Thessalonians had received Paul's message as the word of God (*1 Thess.* 2:13) and evidently accepted without question his role as an apostle of the Lord Jesus.

THE READERS DESCRIBED

Paul addresses the believers in Thessalonica as 'the church of the Thessalonians in God the Father and the Lord Jesus Christ'. In calling them 'the church of the Thessalonians' he is almost certainly using terminology from his rich Jewish heritage. The term 'church' (Greek *ekklesia*, 'assembly') is used about a hundred times in the Greek translation of the Old Testament to refer to Israel as God's congregation. Gathered before him as his worshipping, obedient, servant people, Israel formed God's 'church', or his assembly. The Thessalonians now belonged to that assembly. Gentiles though they largely were, through believing the gospel they had become God's people. They were a true expression of his worshipping community in the city of Thessalonica.

Their special character as an assembly of God's people is further strengthened when Paul describes them as 'in God the Father and the Lord Jesus Christ'. The term *ekklesia* was in common use throughout the Greco-Roman world, and the Thessalonians would have been very familiar with it. Public gatherings to transact civil affairs in towns and cities were called assemblies, the same term Paul now uses to describe the church in Thessalonica. However, the Thessalonians could be assured that their assembly was totally different from all others. It was in God the Father and the Lord Jesus Christ. It had its origin and life in God the Father and in the Lord Jesus. It belonged to God and was in living union with him. To a young church facing persecution, this assurance must have brought great comfort.

Churches today need to remember that this is their identity, too. When tempted to follow the trends of secular organisations or facing threatening crises, their leaders in particular need to recall that the church is in God the Father and the Lord Jesus Christ. It belongs to God, is governed by God, and has its resources in God.

THE BLESSING SOUGHT

Paul closes his introduction with the words 'Grace and peace to you'. A non-Christian contemporary would have used a single word, 'Greeting' (*charein*). For Paul, however, the gospel had introduced believers into a totally new world, a world not characterised by good wishes but by spiritual blessings in Jesus Christ. In Christ they received God's grace, his undeserved favour and mercy. They received the forgiveness of their sins, a new standing with God, the continued supply of all their needs through the Holy Spirit, and a glorious future destiny (*Eph.* 1:3ff.). And because of this, they now experienced true peace. They knew what it was to live in harmony with God and to enjoy the inner tranquillity that comes from being made whole by him.

The Thessalonians had already experienced these great gospel blessings. Nevertheless, Paul longed for them to experience these in an ongoing and even deeper way. Their life as a church in God the Father and in the Lord Jesus Christ entitled them to the constant blessing of grace and peace.

This is the privilege and need of all Christians today. Grace and peace sum up the riches we have in Christ. We should seek them above all else because having these, we have everything we need.

2

Giving Thanks

²We always thank God for all of you, mentioning you in our prayers. ³We continually remember before our God and Father your work produced by faith, your labour prompted by love, and your endurance inspired by hope in our Lord Jesus Christ (1 Thess. 1:2–3).

A spirit of gratitude shines through Paul's letters. He knew that he personally had much to be thankful for. He had once been a misguided, self-righteous persecutor of the church, deserving God's severest wrath. Instead, he had received his love (*1 Tim.* 1:12–14). What could he be but thankful?

But he was thankful not only for the grace that he himself had received. He had a keen eye for it in the lives of others as well. He knew that every sign of true spiritual life could be traced back to the mercy of God. And wherever he saw those signs, he was quick to praise God for them.

The Thessalonian Christians gave Paul and his companions, Silas and Timothy, good reason to thank God. Though prematurely deprived of their founding preachers, they had not only survived in difficult circumstances but thrived under them. They had held true to Christ and grown in faith and love. When Timothy brought Paul news of this, the apostle could scarcely contain his joy (*1 Thess.* 3:6,9). On that note he begins his first letter to them.

MEN OF PRAYER

'We always thank God for all of you', he writes, 'mentioning you in our prayers.' In all likelihood, Paul the Christian kept up the practice of regular hours of prayer learned as Saul the Jew. If that were the case, he would have prayed at least three times a day. And it would appear that never a prayer session passed without the apostle and his companions thanking their God and Father for the whole Thessalonian church.

In this way he assures his readers at the outset of his letter that they are never out of his mind. The length of his absence and the taunts of unbelievers might have raised doubts in their minds about this. But Paul puts any such fears to rest. He and Silas and Timothy always kept the Thessalonians before them and always in the best of ways. They were constantly thanking God for all of them in their prayers.

To pray so regularly and so selflessly is never easy. Yet prayer of this sort lay at the heart of Paul's ministry. His effectiveness as a preacher and a pastor can never be separated from his prayerfulness. If we are to see anything approaching his fruitfulness in our ministries, we must recapture his faithfulness in our prayers.

CAUSES FOR THANKS

Paul and his companions did not thank God in just a vague or general way for the Thessalonians. Rather, three things in particular came to mind as they thought of them in prayer: their work produced by faith, their labour prompted by love, and their endurance inspired by hope in our Lord Jesus Christ (v.3).

(i) Life in the Thessalonian church was marked by work produced by faith. When the gospel came to these people they did not receive it as a set of ideas to be talked about and debated. It had changed their whole outlook and way of life. The true and living God became the centre of their existence. They now lived for him in the power of his Spirit as they waited for his Son to return from heaven (vv.9–10). They were no longer caught up in their own self-interest and enslaved by their sinful desires, but cared for one another and for those still in idolatry and ignorance round about them. Their new life was one governed in every way by their faith in the gospel. And as Paul, Silas and Timothy thought of this, they overflowed in thanks to God for the great work he had done among them through their ministry.

The gospel will always revolutionise lives where it is truly believed. It gives people a new centre for life, a new motive for life, and a new power for life. That being so, professions of faith not followed by changed lifestyles must be considered suspect. Faith without works is indeed dead (*James* 2:26).

(ii) A second feature of church life in Thessalonica was labour prompted by love. The new way of life that followed conversion had been costly for the believers. The works born of faith had required toil to the point of weariness, often at great personal expense. They had discovered that their new life in God the Father and the Lord Jesus Christ (v.1) called for labour rather than leisure and had unhesitatingly embraced that demand out of love.

Love had been the constraining force behind their service to one another. Upon hearing and believing the gospel, they had experienced a strange new selfless concern for others that made them willing and glad to lay down their lives for them. It was this that had produced the shining instances of costly self-giving that thrilled the hearts of Paul, Silas and Timothy. The love of Christ in us will always do that.

(iii) Then thirdly, the missionaries thanked God for the endurance inspired by hope in the Lord Jesus Christ that they had witnessed in the Thessalonians. Their faith in the gospel and the new life that flowed from it had brought suffering upon them (v.6). From the beginning their commitment had been put to the sternest test. However, they had held steadfastly, enduring the worst their opponents could hurl at them.

They had done so not simply out of natural courage, but out of a stamina inspired by their confidence in the coming of the Lord Jesus Christ. The gospel Paul had preached had declared that Jesus would return to save his people and to judge the world (v.10). This future event burned as a living hope in their hearts, inspiring them to press on, counting no trouble too much to bear.

Eager expectation of the Lord's return and the glory to come has proved in the past, and remains still today, the primary source of patient endurance in trial. Sadly this joyful hope does not always glow as brightly in the church today as it must.

LESSONS TO BE LEARNED

These three features of the church in Thessalonica stirred Paul, Silas and Timothy to thank God constantly. We may be sure that their prayers were far from lifeless. A keen awareness of spiritual blessings prompts fervent prayer and praise. We often fail to thank God as we should because we fail to see how good he has been to us. Our private and corporate worship would be transformed if we took more time to reflect on the blessings he has showered upon us.

The Thessalonians also help us to understand the source of vigorous, active, steadfast church life and Christian living. They were a working, labouring, enduring group of Christians. Any pastor would love to have church members like them! What lay behind this striking display of life? Not programmes, superb organisation, or management techniques. Rather, it was the faith, love and hope produced by belief in the gospel.

At heart, the greatest need of the Christian church in every age is for a continuous experience of the power of the gospel. Reliance upon anything less will always create a house of straw that will not stand the test of time or survive the scrutiny of God's judgement (*1 Cor.* 3:12–15).

3

God's Chosen People

*⁴For we know, brothers loved by God, that he has chosen you,
⁵because our gospel came to you not simply with words, but also
with power, with the Holy Spirit and with deep conviction. You
know how we lived among you for your sake. ⁶You became
imitators of us and of the Lord; in spite of severe suffering, you
welcomed the message with the joy given by the Holy Spirit.
⁷And so you became a model to all the believers in Macedonia
and Achaia* (1 Thess. 1:4–7).

Paul has not finished with the theme of thanksgiving yet. In fact,
verse 4 is properly still part of the sentence he began in verse 2.
We have seen that the apostle and his missionary companions, Silas
and Timothy, always thanked God for the Thessalonians as they
called to mind their work produced by faith, their labour prompted
by love, and their endurance inspired by hope in the Lord Jesus
Christ (v.3). But these were not the only things that stimulated their
praise.

These vigorous signs of spiritual life pointed to a deeper truth.
They were a sure sign to the missionaries that God had chosen their
converts in Thessalonica to be his people, a truth confirmed by the
way in which the gospel had come to them and been received by them
(vv.4–7). This was reason above all others to be thankful.

CHOSEN PEOPLE

In assuring the believers in Thessalonica that they have been chosen
by God (v.4), Paul is again revealing his deep spiritual roots. The
idea that God chooses or elects people is embedded in the Old

Testament. Moses, for example, reminded the Israelites before they crossed the Jordan into the Promised Land that they had been chosen and set apart from all other nations to be God's treasured possession (*Deut.* 7:6).

Believers in Christ in the New Testament are God's chosen people in this same way. They have been chosen before time in Christ to be sons of God and heirs of glory (*Eph.* 1:4, *Rom.* 8:17). That is why Paul can address the Thessalonians as 'brothers loved by God'. In Christ they are together members of one family and the objects of God's special love. The term 'brothers', while expressing endearment and affection, more importantly indicates kinship in the family of God.

Small wonder, then, that Paul thanks God for the Thessalonians. Through his grace they have become brothers and sisters in the Lord. They were once strangers to the promises and household of God (*Eph.* 2:19) but are now his people, destined to share in the glory of Christ (*2 Thess.* 3:14).

This is how all Christians should think of themselves. If we are true believers, we are not simply people who have been freed from a burden of sin and guilt. This is true, of course, but it is only part of the picture. We are now God's children and his heirs. And as such we ought to be profoundly thankful to him and deeply affectionate to one another.

POWERFUL PREACHING

But how could Paul and his co-workers be so sure that the Thessalonians were God's chosen people? Their flourishing spiritual life noted earlier (v.3) would have given them grounds for this confidence. But the way the gospel had come to them and been received by them provided added confirmation.

Paul knew that God called his chosen people to faith through the gospel (*2 Thess.* 3:14), and he had seen that gospel at work in Thessalonica in ways that left no doubt in his mind that God was calling people to himself there. For their gospel, the message that he, Silas and Timothy preached, had come not simply with words, but also with power, with the Holy Spirit and with deep conviction (v.5).

Several things in this remarkable statement need to be considered.

(i) The gospel had come to the Thessalonians in word. The three missionaries had passed on the good news of God's grace in Christ in their preaching. They had reasoned with Jews in the synagogue and taught others the message as well (*Acts* 17:1–5). Preaching is important. Without it, people cannot hear and believe (*Rom.* 10:14).

(ii) Preaching as the mere human activity of speaking the gospel in words is not all that counts in people coming to saving faith. The point Paul makes here is that the preaching at Thessalonica had not been in word only, but also with power. While this may refer to miracles accompanying the ministry of the word, it is more likely that the apostle is saying that the message had a special force about it that made it effective in the lives of people as they listened.

(iii) This power was connected with the ministry of the Holy Spirit. He was the source or agent of this special convicting influence (*John* 16:8). Paul was deeply aware of the ministry of the Spirit in this regard. When he preached he did not rely on his own ability with words to create effect, but on a demonstration of the Holy Spirit's power (*1 Cor.* 2:4). He knew that only God could open the minds of sinful people to understand and believe the gospel, and he relied totally upon the Spirit to use his plain preaching of the cross of Christ as a vehicle for this mighty work.

(iv) Evidently, Paul, Silas and Timothy were fully aware that the Holy Spirit was at work through them as they preached in Thessalonica. The testimony of their hearts convinced them that something more than mere speaking was taking place. As they spoke, they felt a deep conviction within themselves that they could attribute only to the Holy Spirit. They were given a deep sense of the certainty of their message, boldness to proclaim it, and confidence that it would be effective. Together these things convinced them that God was at work through them calling people to himself in Macedonia's capital city. This made them sure that their converts there were indeed brothers, loved by God and chosen.

Paul's experience in Thessalonica remains a model for gospel preaching in our generation. It reminds us that ultimately it is the gospel itself that God uses to save people (*Rom.* 1:16). Again, it teaches us that effective preaching of that gospel depends entirely on the work of the Holy Spirit. We must constantly re-learn our need of the Holy Spirit in evangelism and Christian ministry. Without his presence our efforts are fruitless. And if he is not working through us, we must ask why this is the case. Is he being hindered by our prayerlessness, our self-reliance, or our sinfulness? Powerless Christian witness should be intolerable to us.

RADICAL RESPONSE

Yet another aspect of the preaching event in Thessalonica assured Paul that his readers were God's children. It was their response to the message.

Upon hearing the gospel, those who welcomed it were radically changed. They became imitators of Paul and his companions and, through them, of the Lord (v.6). Knowing how their preachers lived (v.5), they took their stand with them and patterned their lives after them. It cost them severe suffering to do so, but even this could not smother their joy given by the Holy Spirit (v.6). Such a radical transformation and such superhuman joy could mean only one thing to Paul. God had been at work, and these were his people.

A changed life is still the best evidence that we have become Christians. Many rely heavily upon their inward feelings and moods or on past spiritual experiences for assurance that they have eternal life. Feelings and frames of mind can change, however, and experiences can be deceptive. A radically new lifestyle, coupled with the inward joy of the Holy Spirit, is much safer ground upon which to rest our hopes.

Others will be encouraged when they see such changes in us. This was the case with the Thessalonians. News of their conversion soon reached all the believers in the provinces of Macedonia and Achaia (v.7). So deeply impressed were they with what they heard that they began to look to the Thessalonians as a model for their own lives. Likely as not they were all facing the same sorts of trials as the Thessalonians, but perhaps not with the same courage. Here was this young church suffering so much, yet holding true to the faith with such joy. What an inspiration it was!

Do people react like that when they see our lives? Inspirational example does have a place in the Christian community (*1 Tim*. 4:12). Do our lives challenge fellow Christians to greater holiness, boldness and perseverance?

4

A Missionary Church

[8]The Lord's message rang out from you not only in Macedonia and Achaia – your faith in God has become known everywhere. Therefore we do not need to say anything about it, [9]for they themselves report what kind of reception you gave us. They tell how you turned to God from idols to serve the living and true God, [10]and to wait for his Son from heaven, whom he raised from the dead – Jesus, who rescues us from the coming wrath (1 Thess. 1:8–10).

News of the arrival of the gospel in Thessalonica soon spread far and wide. There was nothing secretive about the company of people who had received it and remained loyal to it after its messengers had been forced to leave the city. On the contrary, the church in Thessalonica became a beacon of spiritual light in a world of pagan darkness.

It became, in other words, a missionary church. In that sense it provides a pattern for us still today. The Lord Jesus Christ wants his church in every generation to take the gospel to the whole world. How did the Thessalonians do so? What was it that made their witness so effective?

EFFECTIVE WITNESS

That their witness was effective is vividly clear. Paul says that the Lord's message – the gospel that he, Silas and Timothy had preached (v.5) – rang out from the Thessalonians. They became a sounding board, as it were, continually bouncing the message outwards in all directions. News of their faith in God not only echoed throughout the whole of Macedonia and the neighbouring Roman province of Achaia, but it became known everywhere.

How did this come about? It may be that the Thessalonian Christians, upon accepting the word, patterned themselves upon the apostle and his helpers (v.6) and became preachers of the gospel in Thessalonica and its surrounding towns and villages. They must have recognised that the news that had so changed their own lives could not be kept to themselves. A genuine experience of God's grace always compels us to share it with others.

Even if they did not become preachers in this sense, their transformed lives must have spoken loudly to others. Husbands must have been astounded by the way their converted wives now acted. Relatives and friends were probably both perplexed and amazed at the changes that they saw in their former companions in revelry. Travellers passing through the busy port city would hear about these things and gossip reports at their various stopping points. In this way news of what had happened in Thessalonica would soon spread.

All of this contributed greatly to Paul's ongoing missionary work. When he and his companions arrived in a new place, they did not need to mention their visit to Thessalonica (v.8). News of this event was so well known that people themselves could report what kind of reception the missionaries had received there. Presumably this made them the more eager to hear what the missionaries had to say.

RADICAL CONVERSION

What had people heard about the apostle's visit to Thessalonica?

(i) They had heard, firstly, that as a result of it some of the Thessalonians had turned to God from idols (v.9). This in itself must have been startling news. Idolatry had such a grip on people that they dreaded causing the least offence to any of their numerous deities. Religious life was a constant process of placating angry gods and courting their favour. To abandon them was sure to provoke the full force of their vengeance and bring recriminations from terrified family and friends as well. Yet the Thessalonian Christians had done just that. They had turned from their idols to God.

(ii) Secondly, they had decided to serve the living and true God (v.9). They had not merely attached themselves to a new object of ritual worship but entered into a relationship with a living and personal Being. That relationship called for total devotion and a complete reorientation of life. Believers in the living God were now his glad servants, dedicated to discovering and doing his will.

This revolution is what Christians call conversion. It is much more than believing ideas and making resolutions. At heart it is a transfer of allegiance from idols to God. Idols need not be figures of wood or stone. Essentially anything that claims God's right to our total devotion is an idol. The quest for wealth and power is a modern form of idolatry. So too are selfish ambition, obsession with sport, infatuation with people, and addiction to drugs, sex or food. Conversion means turning from these to the living God. It also means making a radical commitment to please him in everything.

Change of this sort witnesses powerfully to the gospel. It often speaks far more loudly than words. What is more, it generally creates opportunity for words. Almost always effective evangelism is connected with witness in both word and life. Missionary churches are churches which both tell and show the gospel.

Are our lives still crippled by idols? Are unbelievers challenged by the single-mindedness of our devotion to God and determination to serve him? Perhaps failure at this point is stunting our personal witness and hindering modern evangelism at large.

EAGER HOPE

(iii) But the change that took place in the Thessalonians contained a third element. Not only did converts exchange their allegiance and experience a reorientation of their lifestyles; they also became gripped with eager anticipation.

Having turned to the living God, they began to wait for his Son from heaven (v.10). Paul's gospel centred on Jesus Christ, the Son of God. It declared not only that he died for the sins of his people according to the Scriptures (*1 Cor.* 15:3), but that God raised him from the dead as a demonstration that he was indeed his Son (*Rom.* 1:4). This Jesus, Paul taught, had been exalted above all other powers and now reigned from heaven as Lord and Christ (*Phil.* 2:9–11). This he would continue to do until he returned to judge the peoples of the earth and bring this present age to an end.

It was to this return of the Lord that the Thessalonians looked with such eagerness. They knew that it would be an awesome and dreadful occasion, a spectacle of divine wrath and judgement. But they also knew that as believers they could say that Jesus rescues us from the coming wrath (v.10). His faithful disciples would not be condemned at his return but ushered into the glorious freedom of the children of God (*Rom.* 8:21).

The expectation of these great events captivated the minds and hearts of the early Christians. They did not think of them as remote future events but anticipated them in their own lifetime. It filled them with such eager hope that some apparently even stopped working to wait for their fulfilment (4:11,12, *2 Thess.* 3:6–15).

With the passing of centuries, the return of Jesus has lost some of its immediacy in the minds of Christians. Along with that it has faded as a prominent element of the gospel. It once shaped the outlook of Christians and raised them on tiptoe in anticipation. But for many today it is little more than a climactic finale reserved for a day in the perhaps still distant future.

This should not be the case. The Christian gospel is not only about personal salvation from sin and its consequences, important though these are. It announces the mighty acts of God in Jesus Christ to restore all things to himself (*Col.* 1:20). If we truly believe that God is the Lord of history and that the return of his Son will signal the renewal of all things, we, like the Thessalonians, will eagerly wait for him to come from heaven.

5

A Genuine Ministry

¹You know, brothers, that our visit to you was not a failure. ²We had previously suffered and been insulted in Philippi, as you know, but with the help of our God we dared to tell you his gospel in spite of strong opposition. ³For the appeal we make does not spring from error or impure motives, nor are we trying to trick you. ⁴On the contrary, we speak as men approved by God to be entrusted with the gospel. We are not trying to please men but God, who tests our hearts. ⁵You know we never used flattery, nor did we put on a mask to cover up greed – God is our witness. ⁶We were not looking for praise from men, not from you or anyone else (1 Thess. 2:1–6a).

Paul was never one to rush to his own defence for selfish reasons. But whenever the gospel was at stake or the welfare of churches was threatened on his account, he did not hesitate to defend his integrity or authority.

This next section (2:1–3:17) is best understood as such a self-defence or self-vindication. While we cannot reconstruct the circumstances in Thessalonica definitely, it seems that the reputation of Paul, Silas and Timothy had come under fire after they had left the city. Opponents of the young church were trying to undermine the gospel by slandering its messengers. If they could smear the character of its preachers, then they could cast doubts on its message. In this way, Christian converts might be retrieved and the unwelcome church dissolved.

Two aspects of the apostolic ministry seem to have come under attack. One was the integrity of the missionaries themselves. Were they genuine teachers, or were they, like many self-appointed philosophers who travelled the Egnatian Way, men who were acting out of self-interest? Were they trying to help people or exploit them?

Secondly, how much did they care for those who did believe them? Since they had fled the city there had been neither sight nor sound of them. They were fly-by-nights, people seemed to be saying, men who thought more of their own safety than of their message or those who received it.

Concern over how these slanders might affect the church in Thessalonica stirred Paul to respond. He refutes first the challenge to their ministry (2:1–16), then the challenge to their care (2:17–3:13).

COURAGEOUS PROCLAMATION

How does Paul respond to the accusation that he, Silas and Timothy were just self-interested charlatans?

(i) He does so firstly by appealing to what the Thessalonians themselves know of them. He does not try to win the point by mere argument, but looks rather to eyewitness evidence to prove his case. The Thessalonians knew better than anyone that their visit to the city was not a failure (v.1). They had come with a sincere purpose and design. The Thessalonians had seen how the three men had lived among them for their sake (1:6) and had ample opportunity to verify their motives and message. The last thing that could be said about them, if only the Thessalonians thought about it, was that they were shiftless vagrants without anything of substance to offer.

(ii) Secondly, Paul points to the circumstances surrounding their coming to Thessalonica as proof of their genuineness. They had not strolled into the city as relaxed and overfed tourists. They had entered still sporting the scars of woeful mishandling in Philippi. There they had suffered and been mistreated shamefully on account of the gospel (v.2). They had been arrested on the charge of causing mayhem in the city (*Acts* 16:20,21); they had been beaten and imprisoned without a fair trial. Treatment like this would have been enough to stop any phoney mission in its tracks.

But none of this had deterred Paul, Silas and Timothy. Upon arriving in Thessalonica from Philippi, they dared to tell the gospel of God. With the help of God, they spoke freely and boldly in spite of strong opposition (v.2). That opposition may have come from within their own hearts – Paul uses a term here that resembles our English word 'agony,' and may be suggesting that it cost them inner anguish to face bristling audiences again. More likely, however, he is referring to the violent opposition they faced from the Jews in Thessalonica. His point is that in spite of danger and severe struggle, they nevertheless kept on preaching. And what did this show but their deep sincerity? Theirs was clearly not a ministry without strong purpose and value.

Christians who serve out of a sense of conviction and call persevere no matter how difficult their circumstances. God strengthens them to stick at their posts. Those acting out of self-interest, however, tend to falter when the going gets tough. Stickability, especially in times of difficulty and opposition, is a proof of genuineness.

GODLY MOTIVATION

What was it that enabled these men to preach under such threatening conditions? What drove them from one city to another and made them put themselves at such risk?

Paul can say first that it had nothing to do with false or fleshly motives. The appeal that they made – and it must be noted that their preaching was in the form of a persuasive appeal aimed at gaining a response – did not spring from error or impure motives, nor were they trying to trick their hearers (v.3). Their preaching did not originate from myth or speculative reasoning; neither was there any hint of either self-interest or deceit. Apparently travelling teachers in the first century commonly used their influence as a means of sexual exploitation. But this was not the case with Paul and his companions. The Thessalonians themselves knew how holy, righteous and blameless the three men had been while they were among them (2:10).

Flowing from that, there was nothing about their ministry designed to beguile or trick people. The sham philosophers of Paul's world often used devious means to gain popularity and wealth. Not so the apostle and his helpers. Such mean motives could never have sustained them and were certainly not what lay behind their preaching, say what their opponents might about them.

Rather, Paul preached out of a deep sense of responsibility to God. Why had he, Silas and Timothy dared to preach the gospel in Thessalonica after being so abominably treated in Philippi? Because they knew they were men approved by God to be entrusted with the gospel (v.4). They saw themselves as privileged stewards (*1 Cor.* 4:1) of a very valuable item – the message of the gospel. They had been entrusted with its care and charged with the task of preaching it faithfully. Aware of this solemn responsibility, they spoke not with an eye to pleasing men, but with a deep sense of being under the scrutiny of God who tested their hearts (v.4). Three things – the thought of being approved by God (tested and endorsed by him), trusted by God, and constantly searched by God – banished any possibility of dishonesty from their hearts and stirred them to fearless, persistent gospel preaching.

Nothing provides a better check to self-seeking in Christian ministry than a constant awareness of God. If we see our tasks as given by him and realise that our actions are always before him (*2 Cor.* 2:17), we will be kept from impurity, insincerity and slackness in our work for him.

ABOVE-BOARD METHODS

What is more, we will be kept from all taint of shady practice in what we do for him. Writing to the Corinthians some years later, Paul could say that he had 'renounced all secret and shameful ways' and that he did not 'use deception, nor . . . distort the word of God' (*2 Cor.* 4:2). He chose instead to present the gospel plainly in the power of the Holy Spirit (*1 Cor.* 2:5).

This had been his approach in Thessalonica. The believers there were again witness to the fact ('you know', v.5) that he had never used flattery in his preaching. He had avoided using fair words for selfish or greedy ends. He had renounced all slick speaking that might lull listeners into a false sense of trust. Because he was not seeking to line his pockets or attract a personal following (of this God was witness), his speaking was never a mask to cover up greed or a means to win the praise of men (vv.5–6a). Anything shady was anathema to Paul. The Thessalonians themselves could verify this from their knowledge and experience.

Paul's jealous concern to avoid all that faintly resembled manipulation is a powerful lesson to us. In contrast to what we often see today, his was a remarkably plain and transparent ministry. While plainness in itself is not necessarily a virtue in Christian ministry, transparent simplicity is. As God's servants, tested by him, approved by him, trusted by him, and watched by him, how can we be anything but honest?

Methods do count. Anything that misleads and anything that serves personal popularity and wealth comes under God's ban.

6

A Gentle Ministry

⁶ᵇAs apostles of Christ we could have been a burden to you, ⁷but we were gentle among you, like a mother caring for her little children. ⁸We loved you so much that we were delighted to share with you not only the gospel of God but our lives as well, because you had become so dear to us. ⁹Surely you remember, brothers, our toil and hardship; we worked night and day in order not to be a burden to anyone while we preached the gospel of God to you (1 Thess. 2:6b–9).

'Actions speak louder than words,' the familiar saying goes. Paul seems to have believed that. When the integrity of his ministry came under fire he did not rely on fine speeches to win his case. Instead, he told people to look at his lifestyle and the general manner of his ministry. These provided the most convincing proof that he and his co-workers were indeed genuine servants of Christ and not manipulative deceivers out to make money for themselves.

Opponents in Thessalonica, it would seem, had been casting a slur on Paul's sincerity. They were probably claiming that he was out to take advantage of those who followed him. He has already assured the Thessalonians that his motives were pure and his methods above board (2:3–6). Now he reminds them of how gentle he and his helpers, Silas and Timothy, were while with them. Far from exploiting them as money-seeking bullies, they had lived among them as tender and caring parents.

UNBURDENSOME

As an apostle, Paul might well have made heavy demands upon the new believers in Thessalonica. This, however, was not Paul's pastoral style (vv.6b–7a). Paul here associates Silas and Timothy with himself as apostles. Most likely he is using the term in a more general sense here (cf. *Rom.* 16:7) to refer to those who have been entrusted by Christ with the task of establishing his church. His point is that as envoys of the Lord Jesus himself, they held a position of particular honour. And having such, it was within their power to make demands on the Thessalonians. One way or another they might have made life more difficult for them.

They were careful, however, not to be a burden to them (v.6a). The expression 'to be a burden' means literally 'to add weight'. It can refer to burdensome commands or duties laid upon people by an authority figure. It can also refer to burdens associated with providing food and shelter and financial remuneration. Paul uses the term most often in this latter sense when writing to churches. He did everything in his power to avoid making his material maintenance a matter of concern to the churches he was serving (cf. *2 Cor.* 11:9; 12:14).

Here Paul uses this fact as an added proof that his ministry among the Thessalonians had not been self-seeking. Had he and his companions been interested only in personal gain they would not have hesitated in making heavy demands upon the new believers. False teachers infiltrated the church in Corinth and enslaved, exploited, and took advantage of Christians there (*2 Cor.* 11:20). But such ruthless, self-seeking exploitation would have been abhorrent to Paul and a contradiction to the gospel he preached.

The temptation to use rank for personal gain is an ever present one. Christian leaders must resist it valiantly. Office within the church is something to be valued but never abused.

TENDER

Rather than imposing a heavy burden upon the Thessalonians, Paul, Silas and Timothy had been gentle among them (v.7). They had acted toward them like a mother caring for her little children. There was nothing harsh or autocratic about their ministry. They had shown instead the devotion of a mother, or a nurse, cherishing her little children.

There is some question as to whether the original text has the word for 'babes' rather than 'mother' (or nurse) as it is in our translation. The idea then would be that Paul and his helpers came right down to the level of the Thessalonians, as children speaking to children, in their service among them. Or perhaps it might mean that, as little children, there was a complete absence of deceit in their behaviour.

It does seem better, however, to see a contrast here between the 'weighty' (burdensome) ministry that the apostles might have exercised as representatives of Christ, and the gentle, motherly one that they did. Few images express the idea of gentleness better than that of a mother nursing, warming, and cherishing her own children. And if that was the character of their ministry, it made a lie of claims that the apostles were simply using the Thessalonians for their personal advantage.

The sincerity of their love for them is expanded in the words that follow (v.8). Paul and his companions had developed an intense affectionate yearning for the believers in Thessalonica. Theirs was no professional relationship, but one of deepest personal intimacy. While they were eager above all things to share the gospel of God with them, they could not but be drawn to share their own selves as well.

By this, Paul may have meant that he, Silas and Timothy were ready to die for the Thessalonians (*1 John* 3:16). But more probably he is saying that they wanted to share their inner lives with them, or that they wanted to offer all that they had, mind and body, in their service.

Whatever his meaning, his message is plain. The missionaries were no fake preachers intent on fleecing those they could dupe with fair- sounding words. They were preachers of the truth whose hearts were deeply knit with their converts.

A combination of truth and love is the recipe for all effective evangelism and pastoral work. God speaks and works through his word as it is taught. Yet he also uses the loving hearts of his ministers to melt the coldness of listeners. In this way the gospel is not only told but also shown. Words without the warmth of a loving heart seldom accomplish much.

SELF-SACRIFICING

If recollection of the manner of their ministry was not enough to convince any wavering Thessalonians of the sincerity of Paul and his fellow missionaries, perhaps familiarity with another aspect of the missionaries' actions would. Here was something the new converts could not mistake. They had plenty of opportunity to see with their own eyes the exhausting daily toil that it cost Paul and his friends to provide for themselves (v.9). The words 'toil' and 'hardship' suggest exhaustion and pain respectively. They probably allude to the hard work associated with tent-making and other manual tasks (*Acts* 18:3, *2 Thess.* 3:8). Gifts had reached Paul from the generous but poor church in Philippi (*Phil.* 4:16), but these were obviously not enough to meet the needs of the three men. To make up the shortfall, Paul (and perhaps the other two men as well) had taken up manual labour. It had cost them dearly, but this was a cost they were prepared to pay.

All of this, Paul argues, is clear evidence that he and his companions were not out to delude the Thessalonians. Greed-motivated men would hardly go to such lengths to support themselves while peddling fables. No, the selfless efforts of the missionaries surely witnessed to the fact that their gospel was the gospel of God and that their motives were indeed sincere.

To make the gospel 'without cost' to its hearers ought to be the aim of every Christian institution, church and individual today. Sadly, all too often it becomes a means of gaining wealth.

Furthermore, a self-giving spirit is the mark of a genuine spiritual ministry. Christians should not serve in order to get, be it wealth, power or popularity. They should rather be ready to give in order to serve. The total commitment that is ready to pay in order to serve will call for a second hearing.

7

A Blameless Ministry

[10] You are witnesses, and so is God, of how holy, righteous and blameless we were among you who believed. [11] For you know that we dealt with each of you as a father deals with his own children, [12] encouraging, comforting and urging you to live lives worthy of God, who calls you into his kingdom and glory (1 Thess. 2:10–12).

The strong apologetic or self-defensive tone that has dominated the earlier part of this chapter continues in these verses. Clearly Paul has not finished responding to the accusations that were apparently being levelled at himself and his fellow workers, Silas and Timothy, back in Thessalonica. Reluctant as he was to talk about himself (*2 Cor.* 12:11), he nevertheless found it necessary to do so at length in this letter for the sake of the gospel and the stability of the young church in that city.

We need to note, however, a subtle shift in the issue being addressed in verses 10–12. Earlier Paul has been defending the character of his evangelism (vv.1–9); here it is the nature of his pastoral care. He wants to prove that it was not only his gospel preaching that had been genuine and above board, but also his ministry among the new disciples.

EXEMPLARY CONDUCT

In this matter, Paul appeals to witnesses to support his case. His readers need not rely on his words, true though they would be. They can turn to other sources of evidence.

(i) He appeals first of all to their own knowledge of the way in which he and his helpers had conducted themselves. You are witnesses, he says – or, as it might be paraphrased, 'you of all people know' – how we behaved (v.10). Paul, Silas and Timothy had not kept themselves aloof from their converts in Thessalonica. On the contrary, they had opened their lives to them fully (v.8). His readers had all the evidence they needed in their own experience to refute any charge of apostolic misbehaviour.

(ii) But if that is not enough to convince them, Paul is ready to appeal to a higher witness. In what approaches a solemn oath, he says that God also knows how they had lived among the believing community. He is ready to have his integrity tried by God himself.

These witnesses, he argues, are able to establish that their behaviour among the new believers was holy, righteous and blameless (v.10). When people accepted the gospel, Paul and his helpers did not take advantage of them. No, their conduct among converts was as upright as their gospel preaching had been sincere.

Paul uses three adjectives to describe their pastoral behaviour. It was holy, probably in the sense of being consistently centred upon God and devoted to him. It was righteous, in that it was free from any injustice toward men. And it was blameless, not in the sense of being sinless or perfect, but in being above accusation. Had anyone wanted to lay formal charges against them for wrongdoing, they would have found no grounds for doing so. The preachers of the gospel had been above reproach in the way they lived.

What a striking example of pastoral fidelity Paul provides. And what urgent need there is to imitate him! Opponents of the gospel love to expose the weaknesses of Christians, especially Christian leaders. If they cannot expose the sincerity of their motives and the integrity of their methods, they will call into question the consistency of their characters. How often do you hear the charge, 'Christians are just a pack of hypocrites'? Sadly, sometimes the accusation is merited. Blameless lives, however, would silence these slanders.

FATHERLY CARE

Not content with a general protest of his pastoral integrity, Paul continues by calling upon his readers to remember more precisely the manner of his conduct among them. He likens it to that of a father dealing with his own children (v.11). While he, Silas and Timothy had preached the gospel to them, they lived like nursing mothers towards them (2:7). Then, in their continuing ministry to the new believers, they had acted like caring fathers.

This new metaphor probably reflects what Paul saw to be the complementary roles of mothers and fathers in raising children. Children need not only the tender care and nurture of a mother, but also the example, instruction and correction of a father. The father image retains the idea of deep and tender interest but adds the thought of strong example and firm demand. Remarkably, Paul and his colleagues provided the care of both a mother and a father, creating a pattern for all who are in any way involved with the spiritual nurture of other people.

It is of special interest to note that this paternal care apparently extended to each of Paul's converts individually (v.11). His concern for people went beyond a general care for the collective mass. He took a personal interest in individuals and ministered to them in their homes and in private conversations (*Acts* 20:20).

Nothing proves the genuineness of a ministry more than care for the individual, especially the insignificant individual. It is one thing to address crowds and receive their applause or affirmation. It is another to be committed to a hidden ministry of love that meets people one by one at the point of their need.

In the case of Paul and his helpers, this paternal care had demonstrated itself among the Thessalonians in a threefold way (v.12).

(i) Theirs had been an encouraging ministry. They had been concerned to stimulate the faith of the new converts and to that end had instructed and admonished them in their new way of life in Christ.

(ii) It had also been a comforting ministry, probably in the sense of providing sympathetic support and security in difficulty. Faced as they were with opposition, the new converts were probably in frequent need of the wisdom and comfort of the missionaries.

(iii) But it was also a firm ministry. The missionaries' sympathy did not stop them urging the new disciples to live the costly life of obedience the gospel demanded. Tender as their care had been, it had been tinged with firm demand. Their goal was fervent godliness, not tepid Christianity.

HEAVENLY CALLING

In urging the new believers onwards in their faith, the missionaries were not simply imposing their own demands upon them. Rather, they were helping them live lives worthy of God (v.12). They had preached the gospel to these people (1:5) and seen them turn from idols to God (1:9). The Thessalonians had become God's special people (1:5). Now they needed to live in ways that brought him honour and were befitting his character.

They were to live, furthermore, as those called into his kingdom and glory (v.12). They were people with an incredible destiny. God had made them not only his children, but his heirs as well. They were going to inherit his eternal kingdom – the perfected realm of his rule – and share in his glory. With such a bright future in store, how else could they live? They had to live lives worthy of God.

Paul always had this goal in view when he wrote to Christians. He wanted them to walk worthy of their calling (*Eph.* 4:1). His practical instructions were never bald ethical demands but were simply the inevitable requirements of a new relationship. As God's children, believers are to live to please their Father. As those in union with Jesus Christ, they are to live in the power of his Spirit and not in the strength of the sinful nature (*Rom.* 8:12–13). The new life we have through the gospel demands a new way of living.

A clear grasp of gospel privileges remains the most powerful motive for Christian living and service. The more vividly we see what Christ has done for us, the more likely we are to make progress in godliness and self-denying service. That is why gospel preaching will always prove a better spur to holiness than reciting rules of conduct.

8

The Powerful Word

And we also thank God continually because, when you received the word of God, which you heard from us, you accepted it not as the word of men, but as it actually is, the word of God, which is at work in you who believe (1 Thess. 2:13).

It may be helpful at this point in our study to remind ourselves of Paul's purpose in this part of his first letter to the Thessalonians. In essence, he is encouraging his readers to hold fast to their new faith. He knows that accepting the gospel has brought them stiff opposition. And he knows furthermore that although they have stood up to this well so far, they need encouragement to keep persevering.

One way in which he has tried to encourage them has been through congratulating them on their progress (1:2–10). Another has been to refute slanders against himself, Silas and Timothy by recalling the manner of their preaching and conduct while in Thessalonica (2:1–12). If the Thessalonians took time to reflect on what they knew about the men who had preached the gospel to them, they could not but be convinced that they were entirely trustworthy.

If that was not enough to persade them, then perhaps a reminder of the way in which they had originally embraced the message would settle their minds. Paul has already recalled how, in spite of the severe suffering that came to them, they had received the gospel of God with a joy given by the Holy Spirit (1:6). In 2:13–16 he says more about the way they welcomed the good news. In doing so he provides both a climax to his historical reminiscences and a final compelling reason for remaining true to the faith.

THE WORD OF GOD

Paul introduces this theme in the form of a fresh thanksgiving. Rather than saying, 'Remember the way in which you first responded to our preaching', he tells his readers how he, Silas and Timothy thank God continually for the welcome the Thessalonians gave their message (v.13).

They were especially thankful that the Thessalonian believers had received the gospel as the word of God (v.13). Paul and his companions had arrived in the city claiming to have good news of what the living and true God (1:9) had done through his Son, Jesus Christ. In making this claim they might easily have been dismissed as deluded visionaries. But while some scoffed or mused, the believers among their audience found themselves gripped by the power of the message. Whatever others might think of it, they were persuaded that it was not simply the word of men but the word of God himself. And they accepted it as such gladly (v.13).

What was it that led these people to regard the apostle's teaching as a divine message? Paul does not tell us here in so many words, but we can readily deduce the reason. We may be sure that it was not the eloquence of the preachers, because apostolic preaching was typically plain and direct (*2 Cor.* 4:2). Nor was it likely to be anything ethereal about the content of their message, a message that centred in the death and resurrection of Jesus. The explanation lies in something Paul has already mentioned. He has told us that when he and his companions arrived in Thessalonica and began to preach, they were aware that their words were being accompanied 'with power, with the Holy Spirit, and with deep conviction' (1:5). As they passed on their message, much as a military courier delivers a dispatch, the Holy Spirit was illumining minds and stirring hearts, awakening in people an awareness that God was speaking through these men. In other words, the Holy Spirit was attesting that their message was from God.

While not intentionally aiming to give his readers a lesson on the inspiration of Scripture, Paul's words at this point do witness to the fact that God speaks through men. He reveals his truth to chosen messengers in order that they might transmit it to others – either by word or in writing. The way these messengers express themselves is unique and reflects their personalities and circumstances, but what they say is nevertheless God's word.

This fact reminds us of the importance of preaching the gospel. The gospel is God's word that was entrusted first to the apostles and then through them to the church in all ages. Because it is God's word, it is also 'the power of God to salvation' (*Rom.* 1:16). It pleases God to use that word rather than human wisdom to save men (*1 Cor.* 1:21). Recovering belief in the Bible as God's word and confidence in its power to influence people is the key to renewed effectiveness in evangelism today.

THE WORD AT WORK

The gospel shows itself to be the word of God by the way it transforms people. Paul could speak of that word at work in those who believe (v.13). It was not an empty word, but a living, life-changing word.

It had begun to work in the Thessalonians when they first heard it. Many had been convinced through listening to the Christian preachers that their idols were useless, and they had turned from these to serve the living and true God (1:9). That, as we have already noted, was an incredible turnabout, a change that could be explained only by the fact that God was at work through his word.

But the process of change had not stopped at conversion. Paul stresses that the word of God was continuing to work among those in Thessalonica who believed. Transformation from pagan idolatry to gospel holiness had not happened in an instant. It never does. Sanctification is an ongoing process that takes place through the renewing of our attitudes (*Eph.* 4:23) by the word. As the emptiness and error of our thinking is corrected by the Spirit-empowered word, our lives begin to reflect more of the character of the Lord Jesus (*2 Cor.* 3:18).

In emphasising the power of God's word to change people, it would be wrong to suggest that it always produces results when heard or read. Most of us know only too well how easy it is to read the Bible and listen to preaching without being influenced at all. Paul knew that too, and he is careful here not to imply that the gospel automatically and almost magically produces effects by itself. The expression 'which is at work in you' (v.13) is probably better translated 'which is being made operative among you'. This highlights that it was not the preaching in itself that was accomplishing the work. Rather, the message was being made effective by the Holy Spirit and in this way was becoming the means of renewal.

God's word was working in this way in those who believe; it is believers who experience spiritual change and growth. The Holy Spirit works in our lives firstly by helping us to understand God's word, then by enabling us to believe it, and finally, by stirring us to act upon it. Without heart belief, there will never be true spiritual change.

We must always keep in mind the close tie between spiritual growth and God's word. We cannot hope to make progress in our Christian lives if we ignore the Bible or treat it superficially. God works through his word. And his word must be heard, pondered, welcomed and received before it exercises its life-transforming power within us.

We need to guard on the one hand against undervaluing the power of God's word. It is mighty because it is his word, the word that called heaven and earth into being (*Gen.* 1:3, *Psa.* 33:6) and will one day raise the dead from their graves (*John* 5:28–29). It will surely accomplish the purpose he has for it (*Isa.* 55:11). But on the other hand, it is not automatically effective. We can never presume that merely reading or preaching the word will guarantee results. God's powerful word accomplishes its work only as his sovereign Spirit makes it effective.

9

The Costliness of Believing

*14For you, brothers, became imitators of God's churches in
Judea, which are in Christ Jesus: you suffered from your
own countrymen the same things those churches suffered from
the Jews, 15who killed the Lord Jesus and the prophets and
also drove us out. They displease God and are hostile to all men
16in their effort to keep us from speaking to the Gentiles so
that they may be saved. In this way they always heap up their
sins to the limit. The wrath of God has come upon them at last*
(1 Thess. 2:14–16).

Welcoming the gospel as the word of God had proved costly
for the Thessalonians. It had brought upon them the hostility
of their countrymen (v.14) – presumably their families and neighbours – an experience common to new converts not only in the first
century but ever since.

Far from regarding this kind of persecution as unusual, Paul
looked upon it as evidence of true faith. In the case of the Thessalonians, he saw it as proof that the word of God was at work among
them (2:13). He well knew that when the gospel took root in lives it
inevitably transformed them and brought them into collision with
the unbelieving world in which they lived. That this had happened
in Thessalonica was a good sign, as was the apparent joy and steadfastness with which the converts there bore their sufferings (1:6). It
all contributed to the sense of thankfulness Paul felt for them, and
made him want to encourage them the more.

PARTNERS IN SUFFERING

What was happening in Thessalonica was happening elsewhere, too. In suffering at the hands of their countrymen, the Thessalonians had become imitators of God's churches in Judea who had suffered from the Jews (v.14). They had not set out deliberately to imitate these churches, of course, but they had ended up doing so by sharing their sufferings. Perhaps they also imitated them in the way they bore their afflictions. The shared experience had in effect forged a bond of spiritual union between them. In just the same way, suffering for Christ today brings us into fellowship with the apostles, with the early church, with the prophets, and with the Lord Jesus Christ himself.

Just why Paul should mention the churches in Judea rather than other churches closer at hand is uncertain. Perhaps he wanted his readers to understand that what they were encountering had been the lot of the church from the very beginning. The apostle himself had been a persecutor of the church in Judea in the early days of Christianity and knew all about what it had gone through at that time. The fact that the Thessalonians were now suffering in the same way confirmed that they belonged to the one brotherhood of believers that had its roots in Judea.

In passing we should note the way in which Paul refers to these churches in Judea.

(i) He refers to them as God's churches, that is, churches that belong to God, assemblies of his covenant people.

(ii) He refers to them in the plural as 'churches'. Elsewhere Paul can speak of the church of God as a single body (*Gal.* 1:13). He clearly recognises that the one church of God is the same in essence wherever it expresses itself, making it proper to speak of local congregations as churches of God (cf. *1 Cor.* 1:2).

(iii) He further describes these churches in Judea as in Christ Jesus, probably to distinguish them from Jewish assemblies which also claimed to be congregations of God. Being in Christ Jesus is what makes a group of people a distinctively Christian church.

The churches both in Judea and in Thessalonica had this in common, then, that they suffered from their countrymen. This does not necessarily mean that the persecution in Thessalonica came entirely from the Gentile section of the community. Paul probably has locality rather than ethnic group in mind when he speaks of countrymen. It is highly likely that the Jews in Thessalonica responsible for the first wave of hostility (*Acts* 17:5) continued to stir up trouble for the new community of believers after Paul, Silas and Timothy left. But they would almost certainly have soon been joined in this by the relatives and spouses of Gentile converts. The end result was that the believers, irrespective of whether they had Jewish or Gentile roots, found themselves suffering from their fellow citizens. Often the most intense persecution we suffer as Christians comes from those who have been the nearest and dearest to us.

CONSISTENT OPPOSITION

Mention of the Jews (v.14) diverts Paul into what some regard as an outburst of personal anger and frustration against his countrymen (vv.15–16). He speaks severely of their persistent opposition to the purposes of God and seemingly condemns them for it. On the surface, his feelings towards them appear quite different from those he expresses in his later letter to the church in Rome (*Rom.* 9:2–4; 10:1; 11).

It is wrong, however, to think of these words as an outburst of vindictive passion. Paul did indeed have personal grounds to speak hard words against his own people, given what he suffered from them. But retaliation is not his motive for mentioning them here. He had other reasons for wanting to tell the Thessalonians more about the Jews' history of persecuting faithful believers. The Gentile section of the church must often have wondered why the Jews were so bitterly opposed to the gospel and why, relatively speaking, so few became believers.

They needed to know that the Jews had a history of opposing God and attacking his servants. What happened in Judea was not an isolated event, but one of a series. The Jews had also killed the Lord Jesus and the prophets and, Paul adds, they drove us (Paul, Silas and Timothy) out (v.15). Throughout their history they had repeatedly placed themselves in direct opposition to God, all the time thinking they were serving him. It would have appalled them to know that they were resisting him, but in their stubborn blindness that is exactly what they were doing. They had killed his prophets, crucified his Messiah, and now were hounding his apostles.

In their opposition, the Jews were out of step with both God and man. They displease God and are hostile to all men, Paul writes (v.15). Convinced that they were honouring God, they were in fact displeasing him. And in their efforts to keep Paul and his helpers from speaking to the Gentiles (v.16), they were also proving themselves the enemies of all men. The apostles were custodians of the gospel, the power of God to salvation (*Rom.* 1:16). Apart from their message, there was no way for men and women to be saved. By hindering its preachers, the Jews were in reality committing a terrible crime against humanity.

The same might be said of those who undermine or hinder the spread of the gospel today. We cannot deprive men and women of the words of life without in some sense becoming responsible for the loss of their souls.

INEVITABLE REWARD

The persistent opposition of the Jews to God's purposes had not been without its consequences. In blindly resisting him, Paul writes, they always heap up their sins to the limit (v.16).

This is an expression first found in the Old Testament in connection with the Canaanites (*Gen.* 15:16). It refers to a limit that God in his decree places upon the sins of people. There is a point in sinful behaviour beyond which chastisement or judgement is inevitable.

Paul applies it here to the Jews. In their various acts of rebellion and resistance they had been accumulating their sins up to this appointed limit. They had not been doing so consciously, but this was what had been happening. Their latest efforts to destroy the church and hinder the spread of the gospel were just two more contributions to that stockpile.

Indeed, the limit may already have been reached. This at least is what Paul suggests when he says that the wrath of God has come upon them at last (v.16). The natural meaning of these words is that God's decision to pour out his wrath upon the Jews had already been made. Perhaps the rejection of the Messiah was the final act fixing the nation's fate. Be that as it may, the point of no return had been reached. The consequences of having exceeded the limit might yet be to fall, but the outcome was inescapable.

It is impossible to read these solemn words without feeling a sense of dread. Forbearing as the Lord is, there is a limit to his long-suffering. And when that limit is reached, nothing awaits the impenitent but abandonment to his wrath. How vital it is to be at peace with him through our Lord Jesus Christ (*Rom.* 5:1).

10

Continuing Concern for the Church

^{17}But, brothers, when we were torn away from you for a short time (in person, not in thought), out of our intense longing we made every effort to see you. ^{18}For we wanted to come to you – certainly I, Paul, did, again and again – but Satan stopped us. ^{19}For what is our hope, our joy, or our crown in which we will glory in the presence of our Lord Jesus when he comes? Is it not you? ^{20}Indeed, you are our glory and joy (1 Thess. 2:17–20).

We have noted more than once that Paul, Silas and Timothy were forced to take hurried and premature leave of their new brothers and sisters in Thessalonica (*Acts* 17:10). Both parties had probably hoped that the separation would be brief. But that was not to be the case. Days and then weeks went by without contact of any sort.

It would have been easy in such circumstances for the members of the young church to wonder if they had been forgotten. Perhaps they were being encouraged to think this way by their opponents. Enemies of the gospel might well have been saying that the missionaries were nothing more than another team of self-appointed, fly-by-night itinerant teachers. Teachers of this kind were common at the time. They typically stayed in any one place only as long as it suited them – until they had duped and fleeced their gullible listeners – before heading off to another field for fresh pickings. They cared nothing for their devotees. Their interests were entirely self-seeking.

While we cannot be certain that Paul, Silas and Timothy were being classed among these charlatans, it is very likely that they were.

It would explain why Paul takes such pains (2:17–3:13) to assure the church of the continuing concern he and his associates had for their welfare.

INTENSE FEELING

His words are charged with intense feeling as he takes up this subject, reflecting the depth of emotion that it stirred within him. Addressing them intimately and endearingly, he assures his readers of his longing to see them. His terminology reminds them that he, Silas and Timothy had not deserted them in a stealthy or secretive way. On the contrary, they had been wrenched away from them. Their separation had been unnatural and forced, one that had left them with a sense of desolation and deprivation. They felt like parents bereaved of their children.

This had created an intense longing for the church they had left behind, a passionate, urgent, affectionate desire for their presence. It meant that though absent from them in person, they were never for a moment separated from them in thought or heart. They were always remembering them and praying for them (1:3). This was far from callous, indifferent forgetfulness.

No one could ever accuse Paul of a professional or mercenary spirit. His life was bound up in the welfare of those he served (3:8). He loved them, felt for them, and agonised over them. What an example he provides for Christian workers in every age. And what a rebuke he offers those who serve coldly out of duty, doing their minimal tasks without regard for anything but their own interests. The Christian church needs pastors, elders, leaders and members who care deeply for people.

EARNEST EFFORTS

Paul's care for his spiritual children went further than feelings. It inspired the most earnest practical efforts to return to see them again (v.17). These efforts to return to Thessalonica apparently started a short time after the missionaries had been driven from the city. The wrench they felt in leaving the young and vulnerable church there made them want to return to it just as soon as they could.

There was nothing half-hearted or passing about their attempts to bring about such a reunion. They made every effort to see their friends again, and they persisted in doing so again and again. At least, that was the case with Paul. So deep was his personal concern for them that he makes special mention of it. More than once, indeed, an indefinite number of times, he found himself wanting to come to them and attempting to do so.

Those of us entrusted with the spiritual care of others need to learn from Paul's determination. Do we persist in our efforts to help people when we meet with obstacles, or do we greet them as welcome excuses for not pursuing difficult tasks? Urgent, persistent, passionate effort is all too often missing in pastoral care in the church today. Its restoration would bring immense blessing.

THWARTED PLANS

As earnest as Paul's attempts to revisit the church in Thessalonica were, he found his every attempt to do so blocked. He does not tell us what it was that stood in his way. It may have been a continuing official embargo against his presence in the city. It may have been ill health of some kind (*2 Cor.* 12:7). It may have been persistent opposition from Jews in Thessalonica. Or again, and perhaps more probably, it might have been the local circumstances he found himself facing in Corinth.

Whatever the immediate cause, Paul recognised that Satan lay behind the hindrance (v.18). Every time he tried to return to see the church it was as though he encountered a trench cut across his path. And whatever form that trench took, he knew that it was masterminded by Satan.

Paul understood that he was caught up in a fierce spiritual struggle. He firmly believed that Satan was the leader of a horde of malignant spiritual powers set on resisting the purposes of God (*Eph.* 6:12). Although under the ultimate control of God, this powerful evil spirit nevertheless exercises formidable influence over sinful men and the creation in general – so much so that Paul referred to him as 'the god of this age' and 'the prince of this world' (*2 Cor.* 4:4, *Eph.* 2:2). While not necessarily the direct force behind obstacles, Paul knew him to be the persistent opponent of every attempt to spread the gospel. And he knew that he was meeting him head-on in his attempts to return to help the church in Thessalonica.

Christians often fall into one of two opposite errors in their attitude to Satan. They either treat him as though he does not exist or at least is not a serious threat to the church, or else they become over-absorbed with him and his activities. Paul avoided both extremes. He recognised his power and had a serious regard for his wicked cunning (*Eph.* 6:11–16, *2 Cor.* 2:11), but at the same time he refused to be fascinated by him. He resisted Satan in the power of Christ and urged others to do so, too. We must share this healthy awareness of Satan without being drawn into harmful curiosity about him.

FUTURE GLORY

In spite of these setbacks, Paul's concern for the church in Thessalonica and his desire to return there burned as strongly as ever. What lay behind this? Was it simply his affection for them as people, or his sense of moral obligation to them as the one who had brought their troubles upon them? Or was something deeper stimulating his resolve?

We have already seen how Paul and his colleagues loved the members of the church in Thessalonica (2:7–8). Yet this was not the only thing that aroused their care. They were also driven by a higher sense of duty to Jesus Christ their Lord. They knew that one day they would appear in his presence and give account of their service.

Paul in particular had been entrusted with a very specific commission (*Acts* 9:15). He was to preach the gospel and establish new churches among the Gentiles (*Eph.* 3:8). And what would be the evidence of work well done? Simply this: the Thessalonians and others like them would be in Jesus' presence at his coming (vv.19–20). They would be his hope – the ground of his eager expectation as he stands before his Lord and Judge. They would be the evidence of faithful stewardship and productive labour. They would be his joy and the crown (victor's wreath) in which he would boast – not in a proud or self-interested way, but in a proper, thankful spirit of deep exultation. In them he would see what God had done through him and find his deepest joy and reward.

Little wonder, then, that he was so concerned that his work in Thessalonica should not prove useless (3:5). He was not out to build a kingdom for himself, but he did want to hear his Master say, 'Well done, good and faithful servant' (*Matt.* 25:21). This did not lessen the genuineness of his love for the believers themselves, but it did give an added spur to his efforts to help them.

What motivates our service of others? Is it a feeling of compassion for them? Is it to gain personal satisfaction for a job well done? Is it to be noticed and appreciated? What matters most is that we please the Lord Jesus Christ. One day we shall appear before him and he will test all we have done (*2 Cor.* 5:10). His approval is all that really counts.

I I

A Practical Expression of Concern

¹So when we could stand it no longer, we thought it best to be left by ourselves in Athens. ²We sent Timothy, who is our brother and God's fellow-worker in spreading the gospel of Christ, to strengthen and encourage you in your faith, ³so that no one would be unsettled by these trials. You know quite well that we were destined for them. ⁴In fact, when we were with you, we kept telling you that we would be persecuted. And it turned out that way, as you well know. ⁵For this reason, when I could stand it no longer, I sent to find out about your faith. I was afraid that in some way the tempter might have tempted you and our efforts might have been useless (1 Thess. 3:1–5).

Sincere concern for others expresses itself in more than deep feelings and kind words. It prompts us to find ways of providing practical help as well.

Paul's concern for the Thessalonian believers showed itself in this way. In our last study we noted how he made repeated attempts to revisit them (2:17). Though prevented from doing so, he did not stop his efforts to help. Since a personal visit out of the question, he sent his young assistant Timothy back to see them instead.

PERSONAL SACRIFICE

The decision to send Timothy back to Thessalonica did not come easily. Paul did not resort to it immediately but only when he and those with him could no longer stand the anxiety of not knowing about the church. Only at that point did they decide that it would be best for him to be left and Timothy sent on a return visit (v.1).

Just who was involved in making this decision is hard to determine exactly. Was Paul using an editorial 'we' (really meaning 'I') when he speaks of 'we' being unable to stand it any longer, and 'we' thinking it best to be left alone in Athens? Or was he referring to a smaller or larger group of people? Had both Silas and Timothy, for example, received the message Paul sent back to Berea with those who had escorted him to Athens (*Acts* 17:14,15) and come to join him in that city? If so, then both Paul and Silas, or perhaps even Paul, Silas and Timothy, might have reached the decision together. On the other hand, if only Timothy had returned, then just he and Paul might have consulted about the matter, and Paul remained on his own in Athens after Timothy had left. We do not have the facts to be certain.

But what we do know is that the decision was a costly one for Paul. It resulted, as he puts it, in being left in Athens (v.1). Paul's stay in Athens was not a particularly pleasant one for him. He found the overt idolatry of the city a pressing burden (*Acts* 17:16). Although he preached the gospel there and had opportunity to talk with some of the leading thinkers in the city (vv.18–31), response to the message apparently was limited. The prospect of being left alone in such a city, surrounded by images and confronted by cultured philosophers, did not appeal to him. It left him feeling abandoned and desolate. He would have much preferred to have his young companion, Timothy, with him. Yet he thought it best for the sake of the gospel to send him on this errand and to be left alone.

Sacrifices like this must often be made in Christian service. Love for others calls us to lay down our lives for them (*1 John* 3:16). Often that means the loss of companionship as well as comforts. Many have found that serving Christ means separation from loved ones. Costless ministry is a rarity, if it exists at all.

PASTORAL HELP

The measure of Paul's concern for the Thessalonians is reflected in the person he sent to them. He might well have found a messenger from among the crowds or a few converts at Athens to make a fact-finding visit to Thessalonica. But he did not resort to such an alternative.

Instead, he sent to them Timothy, a brother and God's fellow worker in spreading the gospel of Christ (v.2). Although perhaps a junior member of the missionary team, Timothy was nevertheless a genuine part of it. He was a brother, both a fellow Christian and a treasured spiritual colleague in the ministry. And he was God's fellow worker in spreading the gospel of Christ, one who shared that honour with the apostle Paul himself (*1 Cor.* 3:9). In other words, he was a fully accredited and highly valued member of the team, a fitting representative of Paul and, in fact, of the Lord Jesus Christ.

Timothy's mission was not just that of a news gatherer, although this was definitely part of his brief (vv.5–6). More significantly, he was sent to strengthen and encourage the believers in their faith (v.2). For Paul, the goal of missionary work was not simply getting people to believe the gospel. True faith, where it arose, needed to be nurtured and strengthened. It needed to be corrected when it erred and supplemented when it was weak or inadequate. Timothy was being sent to provide just that kind of ministry. He was not only to observe what was happening in the church, but he was to nurture its faith as well.

Faith lies at the root of the Christian life. It is not only that by which we are saved, but also that by which we live (*Gal.* 2:20, *2 Cor.* 5:7). It can be either weak or strong, sound or defective. No effort should be spared to see that our own faith is vigorous. And what we value for ourselves we should seek for others as well.

PREDICTED SUFFERINGS

What made this nurturing ministry so critical for the Thessalonians was the persecution they were facing. Paul was particularly concerned that none of the converts should be unsettled by the trials they were enduring (v.3). His own experience in the city had made him well aware of the opposition there to the gospel. The new believers had themselves felt the fires of persecution at that time (1:6), and he presumed they had continued to do so since he had left. This is what made his concern for them so unbearable.

It was not that Paul had failed to warn the Thessalonians about the inevitability of suffering. Exactly the opposite was true. They knew quite well that they (as well as Paul and his helpers) were destined to suffer on account of their new faith (v.3). It was something that the missionaries had told them repeatedly (v.4). What is more, these warnings had come to fruition before their very eyes, even while the missionaries were still with them. They had seen what faith in the gospel would bring.

Knowing that persecution is certain does not in itself make its pains any easier to bear. But at least it can keep us from being un-settled, disturbed, or surprised when it does come. Suffering for Christ is no indication that we have gone off track, as it were. Rather, it is proof that we are his true followers and fellow heirs (*Phil.* 1:29, *Rom.* 8:17).

PRESSING CONCERN

The fact of persecution helps us understand the intensity of Paul's concern for the Christians in Thessalonica. It was one thing to be forced to leave these young believers before completing his teaching task. It was another to know that they were facing stiff trials on account of their faith. This is what made the absence and silence so difficult for him to bear, and why he sent someone to find out about their faith (v.5).

We should note that in returning to this point, Paul is not simply repeating what he has already said earlier (v.1).

(i) For one thing, he uses the singular 'I' here, over against the plural 'we' (v.1). This may well be to reinforce the fact that he personally was behind the decision to send Timothy to the church. If, as was suggested in the previous chapter, the ongoing interest of the missionaries was being challenged, these attacks likely centred on Paul, the evident leader of the team. His insistence that he was behind the decision to send Timothy would do much to remove any lingering doubts there may have been of his care for them.

(ii) But secondly, Paul mentions here that he had sent Timothy specifically to find out about their faith (v.5). He not only wanted Timothy to encourage and strengthen their faith, but also to learn how it was faring in such difficult circumstances.

Behind this lay his awareness that the tempter was active in their trials (v.5). Paul knew that their common adversary, the devil, not only tried to prevent the spread of the gospel, but made every effort to pervert and destroy the faith of those who did profess to believe. Persecution was one of his means of achieving that end. And the apostle feared that in this case, he might have succeeded in shaking the faith of his converts, making the missionary effort in Thessalonica useless.

While not for a moment suggesting that true believers can lose their salvation, Paul is nevertheless reflecting the concern that every true pastor should feel for the members of his flock. Skilled spiritual shepherds know that true believers can be deeply shaken and confused in their faith, and to all appearances, draw back from their profession of belief in the gospel for a time. They also know that promising conversions can turn out to be spurious under the heat of trials (*Mark* 4:17). Their concern will always be to see first expressions of faith preserved and strengthened. This was what made Paul so eager to hear news about the Thessalonian church and so willing to send Timothy to them.

12

An Encouraging Report

⁶But Timothy has just now come to us from you and has brought good news about your faith and love. He has told us that you always have pleasant memories of us and that you long to see us, just as we also long to see you. ⁷Therefore, brothers, in all our distress and persecution we were encouraged about you because of your faith. ⁸For now we really live, since you are standing firm in the Lord. ⁹How can we thank God enough for you in return for all the joy we have in the presence of our God because of you? ¹⁰Night and day we pray most earnestly that we may see you again and supply what is lacking in your faith (1 Thess. 3:6–10).

In one of his many wise sayings, Solomon claimed that good news from a distant land is 'like cold water to a weary soul' (*Prov.*25:25). That was how Timothy's report on conditions in the church in Thessalonica must have seemed to Paul. It refreshed him immensely, filled him with gratitude, and fanned into fresh flame his passion to revisit the congregation himself.

TIMOTHY'S GOOD NEWS

Timothy, as we have seen, had been sent to Thessalonica on a fact-finding mission (3:1–2). Paul was desperate to know how the young church there was coping with the opposition it was facing. He feared that the faith of some might have been shaken and his work in the city made of no lasting value. Prevented from visiting the church himself, he had sent Timothy to encourage the believers and to find out what he could about their faith.

Timothy had just returned from that mission and been reunited with Paul in Corinth (*Acts* 18:5). He was able to pass on to Paul an encouraging account of the state of affairs in the congregation. In fact, Paul can write of Timothy bringing 'good news' of their faith and love, a term otherwise restricted to gospel preaching. Timothy's report had fallen on Paul's ears like the good news of the gospel!

(i) That good news concerned, firstly, the faith and love of the Thessalonians. Timothy was able to tell Paul that the believers were holding fast to the truth of the gospel. In spite of what they were suffering, they had not abandoned their new-found belief in the true and living God and in his Son Jesus Christ (1:9–10). What is more, the reality of their faith was evident in lives filled with love (1:3, *Gal.* 5:6). Though Paul would later encourage his readers to grow more and more in their love (4:10), for the moment he rejoices to know that it flourishes among them.

Faith and love are the essence of the Christian life. Through faith, itself a gift from God (*Eph.* 2:9), we come to know God and are brought into the sphere of his empowering grace. And that grace inevitably expresses itself in a life of God-like love (*1 John* 4:7–8). Where the two exist together, they are sure tokens of the saving power of the gospel.

(ii) But Timothy also brought good news of a more personal nature. He told Paul that the church in Thessalonica always had pleasant memories of them and that they longed to see them again, just as the missionaries themselves were eager to see them (v.6). The sudden parting and long absence of Paul, Silas and Timothy, and the slanders of anti-gospel factions in the city, had not dampened the believers' affection for them. They had only the kindliest memories of Paul and his companions and were most eager to see them again.

This was all wonderfully good news to the apostle. How could it be otherwise? True Christian ministry is never impersonal and mechanically task-orientated. It takes place in the context of loving personal relationships formed through costly self-giving. Estrangement always causes deep pain. Fresh assurances of affection, on the other hand, thrill the heart and awaken longings for face-to-face contact.

ITS ENCOURAGING EFFECTS

Timothy's news was a profound encouragement to Paul and those with him. It reached him when he was burdened with his own deep troubles. Missionary activity, never easy at any time, had been particularly difficult in Corinth, it seems. Paul writes of suffering distress and persecution – pressing cares of the strongest sort. These arose in part from the difficulties he faced in Corinth itself and in part from the concern he felt for the churches at large (*2 Cor.* 11:28). It was under the choking burden of these that news of the firm faith of the Thessalonians reached him and cheered him.

In fact, it more than cheered him. It gave him a new lease of life. 'For now we really live,' he writes (v.8). Paul's entire life was bound up in the ministry of the gospel. He lived to see men and women changed by its power and brought into a living bond of faith with the Lord. Nothing disheartened him more than to have people make a profession of faith only to fall from it when allured or opposed by the world. On the other hand, nothing inspired him more than news that his converts were holding firm their faith and making progress in the life of love.

That was the effect of Timothy's report. News that the Thessalonian believers were remaining true to the Lord revived Paul's burdened spirit. He was undoubtedly happy for them and glad for the sake of the gospel witness in Europe as a whole. But he was revived personally as well. The fact that the church was holding true in Thessalonica encouraged him to press on preaching the gospel, freshly assured that his message was indeed the power of God to salvation (*Rom.* 1:16).

News of this sort – of lasting life changes in those we serve in the gospel – is one of the greatest encouragements to press on in difficult times. Difficulties will come and at times threaten to drive us from our work and witness. The recollection of what God has done through us is often enough to keep us at our post and revive our flagging spirits.

PAUL'S INEXPRESSIBLE JOY

The news Timothy brought not only reinvigorated Paul but filled him with joy. This was no mere emotional or psychological response to success, but a spiritual joy experienced in the presence of God (v.9). Since Paul lived in an atmosphere of communion with God, we may presume that his instinctive response to Timothy's report was to pray. Hearing of the steadfastness of his friends in Thessalonica, he undoubtedly lifted his heart to his Father in heaven. And as he did so, he was conscious of being filled with an overflowing and inexpressible holy joy.

This in turn prompted Paul to thank God. He recognised God as the author not only of the persevering faith in the Thessalonians but also of the joy he felt in his own heart. So overwhelming was the experience of that joy that he could not find words to fully express his gratitude. How could he ever thank God enough? (v.9).

Joy is one of the compensating blessings we experience as we suffer in the service of Christ. We may be beaten down and burdened outwardly, yet at the same time be buoyed aloft by an inexpressible inward joy, a foretaste of the glory that awaits us (*1 Pet.* 1:8).

HIS INCESSANT PRAYERS

Finally, Timothy's report stimulated an outburst of fresh energy in prayer. Paul and his companions had always prayed for the Thessalonians (1:2), but fresh news of them added urgency to their intercession. Since Timothy's return, they had prayed for them with a consuming absorption night and day most earnestly (v.10).

Their prayers for the Thessalonians focused on asking God to open a way to see them again. Timothy had brought good news about them, but his report had also revealed that there were things lacking in their faith (v.10). This was understandable, given the short time that the missionaries had been able to stay on their initial visit. Apparently there were truths they did not understand fully, other things they did not know at all, and patterns of living among them that were not consistent with the gospel. Later sections of this letter reveal what some of these were. In other words, there was still much to supply, to mend, to straighten out and set in order. And while Paul knew that a letter could meet some of these needs, he also knew that there was no substitute for face-to-face contact.

He and his friends, therefore, prayed earnestly that God would overcome the obstacles that had until this time prevented a return visit (2:18). Satan had been effectively blocking their path, but they knew that God could overrule their adversary. Their travel plans were ultimately under his control, and prayer was their means of securing his help.

Fervent prayer will always be the outcome of intense pastoral concern. Where it is missing, it points to a crisis of faith and/or to a sad lack of loving concern.

13

A Prayer Wish

*¹¹Now may our God and Father himself and our Lord Jesus
clear the way for us to come to you. ¹²May the Lord make your
love increase and overflow for each other and for everyone else,
just as ours does for you. ¹³May he strengthen your hearts so
that you will be blameless and holy in the presence of our God
and Father when our Lord Jesus comes with all his holy ones*
(1 Thess. 3:11–13).

Almost from the outset of his letter, Paul has been taken up with
assuring the Thessalonians that he, Silas and Timothy have
acted towards them with sincerity and integrity. Presumably he has
been forced to do this to rebut the slanders of opponents.

But now that part of his task is finished. He has provided his
readers with ample evidence to reply to cheap accusations. The
apostle can now press on to deal with other concerns, especially those
that relate to the things lacking in their faith (3:10). But before doing
so, he expresses his thoughts in the form of a prayer, or perhaps
better, a prayer wish.

A CLEAR PATH

Timothy's report on his visit to Thessalonica had renewed an intense
desire in Paul to return and see the church there. It had also driven
him to pray earnestly to that end (v.10).

Now he prays that God would bring that desire to pass. Rather
than presenting a direct request to God, the apostle speaks in a way
that suggests he is expressing a wish. His words, nevertheless, have

the force of a prayer; he wants his God and Father and the Lord Jesus to clear the way for a visit (v.11).

Interestingly, he addresses both the Father and the Lord Jesus in his prayer. Both are viewed as active in responding to his request, and correspondingly, both are addressed in it. Earlier he had identified his readers as the 'church of the Thessalonians in God the Father and the Lord Jesus Christ'(1:1), reflecting his belief that their new life was connected with both the Father and the Lord Jesus. Consistent with that, he now prays to the God who is our Father and to Jesus, who is our Lord.

In doing so the apostle indicates his high view of the person of the Lord Jesus. That he should pray to him as he does to the Father shows that he thinks of him as perfectly united with the Father in every action. In effect, Paul considers Jesus to be equal in dignity and function to the Father. Such consideration would be possible only if he understood that Jesus was essentially one in nature with the Father.

Paul prays that the Father and the Lord Jesus would clear the way for a visit to be made to his friends (v.11). In expressing this wish, he probably has in mind the roadblocks mentioned earlier that Satan had set across his path (2:18). Whatever these were, the apostle looked to God to clear them away. He believed that God's control over the events of life extended even to the practicalities of travel plans and consequently thought it both right and necessary to pray about such things. In doing so he was not abdicating his responsibility to plan and attempt the journey himself. Rather, he was recognising that all the affairs of life are ultimately in the hands of God.

Clinging dependence upon God does not rule out legitimate efforts on our part. But self-effort alone can never guarantee any course of action (*James* 4:13–17).

SUPERABOUNDING LOVE

Paul's primary reason for wanting to revisit Thessalonica was spiritual rather than personal. As much as he wanted to see his new friends there again, he wanted even more to help them grow in their faith. Consequently this, too, finds expression in his prayer for them.

He prays that the Lord would make their love increase and overflow for each other (v.12). They were already a loving community of people (1:3; 3:6; 4:9). Paul was not content, however, with the progress they had made in this respect. He prays that the Lord Jesus would cause their love to increase and overflow, to abound more and more. He has a superabounding measure of love, love that overflows spontaneously and finds practical expression in everyday relationships with others. So central is love to the Christian life that the apostle can elsewhere urge believers to 'live a life of love' (*Eph.* 5:2). The Christian life is about learning to love well!

Yet we cannot do this on our own. By nature we are selfish and unloving, full of 'malice and envy, being hated and hating one another' (*Titus* 3:3). The God-like love that Paul has in mind is a fruit of the Spirit (*Gal.* 5:22). That is why he prays that the Lord would make their love increase. The Lord Jesus himself is the true vine (*John* 15:5), the source of all of our spiritual life through the Spirit. Every spiritual blessing must be sought from him (15:7). A living relationship through prayer with the Lord Jesus is the source of spiritual vigour.

Two other points must be noted in passing.

(i) Paul prays that by the grace of the Lord Jesus, the Thessalonians would overflow with love not only for each other, but for others as well (v.12). The love God creates in our hearts is not a love exclusively for fellow Christians. It is a love as broad as his own, a love that embraces all kinds of people. For the Thessalonians that meant a love that overflowed toward even sceptical pagan relatives and hostile Jewish adversaries. In Jesus' own terms, they were to love their enemies and persecutors (*Matt.* 5:43–48).

(ii) Secondly, note how Paul dares to appeal to his own example in this matter of superabounding love. He prays that the love of his readers might overflow to others 'just as ours does for you' (v.12). This is no empty boast. The apostle has already shown how deeply he, Silas and Timothy cared for the church they had left in such a hurry. The anxious prayers, strenuous efforts, costly absences, and now even this letter, were all expressions of overflowing love. It was this kind of love he wanted them to show as well.

Happy the Christian who can excite others to spiritual growth by inspirational example as well as by persuasive words!

CONFIDENCE IN HIS PRESENCE

Paul wants the Lord Jesus to strengthen the Thessalonians for a definite reason, a reason that he states in the last verse of this chapter. He wants them to be blameless and holy in the presence of our God and Father (v.13).

In speaking of them being in the presence of God, he is thinking of their appearance before him as their Judge. We have already noted more than once Paul's future orientation in his thinking. This is another example of it. He is primarily concerned not about the present but about the future. The Christian has been called by God 'into his kingdom and glory' (2:12), and it is that future hope that dominates the terrain of Paul's thinking. Before we enter the glory and the kingdom, however, we must stand before the Lord to be judged (*Rom.* 14:10). It is this awesome event of which the apostle is thinking here.

He wants his converts to be able to stand in the presence of God blameless and holy. He is thinking not so much of their state when he says this (whether they are in Christ or in Adam), but of their spiritual and moral character. The judgement is concerned with the things done while in the body (*2 Cor.* 5:10). It has to do with moral and ethical character and actions. Paul wants his converts to be able to stand without shame or fear before God. He wants them to be without blame, morally pure, and devoted to the Lord himself.

He knows that their hope of being able to do this rests in the grace of the Lord Jesus. Only as he strengthens their hearts (v.13) – the inner wellspring of their lives – will they be ready to meet God. Biblical holiness is rooted in the heart and expressed in actions. In particular, it is rooted in a heart filled with love, the love Paul has been praying for. Without love we are self-seeking and self-pleasing, invariably guilty of exploiting others rather than serving them. Only a heart overflowing with love to God and man can create the moral stability and purity that will allow us to stand without dread before the great Judge of all.

That awesome event, the apostle adds, will occur when our Lord Jesus comes with all his holy ones (v.13). Jesus himself, in fact, will be the One who judges (*John* 5:22, *Acts* 17:31). In this action, too, there is perfect union between the Father and his Son. We shall appear in the presence of our God and Father even as we stand before the Lord Jesus as our Judge. And this will take place when our Lord comes.

The coming of the Lord is the point of focus to which Paul returns again and again in this letter. For him it marks the end of the old and the consummation of the new. Jesus' return is to be the final coming of God to bring justice and salvation to the earth, and he will come with all his holy ones. This may refer to the heavenly hosts that accompany him as the great warrior returning in final triumph and conquest (*Zech.* 14:5, *2 Thess.* 1:7), to the glorified saints who return to receive their resurrected bodies (*1 Thess.* 4:14), or to both. The point is that the coming of Jesus will be glorious, triumphant and final.

Our Christian lives must be focused on these great future events. It is not a matter of wanting to escape the present and the work that God has for us to do. Rather, it is the way in which our strong confidence in the final purposes of God in Christ is to express itself. If we know Jesus and love him, and believe that God is reconciling all things to himself through him, then we will eagerly wait for his coming.

14

Living to Please God

¹Finally, brothers, we instructed you how to live in order to please God, as in fact you are living. Now we ask you and urge you in the Lord Jesus to do this more and more. ²For you know what instructions we gave you by the authority of the Lord Jesus (1 Thess. 4:1–2).

At this point in his letter Paul's mind turns in a new direction. Up until now he has been countering his critics. Now he begins to counsel his converts.

Timothy's report had alerted the apostle to problem areas, or at least deficiencies, in the congregation in Thessalonica (3:10). Leaders of the church may even have given him a letter for Paul asking for counsel on particular issues. In any case, Timothy's personal recollections would have been sufficient to allow Paul to identify matters that needed attention. From what follows, it appears among the congregation there were unruly elements that needed warning, fearful people who needed encouragement, and weak members who needed supporting (5:14).

Much as he hoped to address these issues in person when a visit became possible, the apostle, good pastor that he was, did not waste time in responding to them. With supreme tact and deep affection he used his pen to address the needs of his flock-at-a-distance.

A 'FINAL' WORD

Characteristically, Paul signals the change of direction in his thoughts with the word 'finally' (v.1; cf. *Eph.* 6:10, *Phil.* 3:1, *2 Thess.* 3:1). This does not necessarily mean that he is coming to the very end of what he has to say. Quite clearly that is not the case in this letter; he might have substituted an expression such as 'and now,' or 'for the rest' to convey what he intended.

But at the same time, the apostle is coming to the final section of his letter. He has written at length about the missionary campaign in Thessalonica, the continuing care that he, Silas and Timothy had for the church, Timothy's visit and his report, and the response that it produced. But he is finished with all of these things now, and he wants to turn to matters relating more directly to their present needs. And since this is the last thing he intends to do, it can properly be said that this is the final section of his letter.

PRACTICAL CHRISTIAN LIVING

The issues that Paul takes up in this closing section are of a practical rather than a doctrinal nature. While, as we shall see, they are closely related to the great doctrines of the gospel, they do not concern them directly. The Thessalonians do not seem to have been bothered by threatening heresies in the same way that the Galatian churches were. Their troubles were connected with the outworking of the gospel in practical Christian life.

Paul begins in a general way by encouraging the church to make further progress in its new way of life. Clearly, he had taught them about the Christian life while with them (v.1). For Paul, missionary work was more than preaching the good news that Jesus was God's Messiah, the Saviour of the world. It also involved instructing new believers how they were to live in order to please God. Jesus, after all, had told his followers that they were both to baptize new disciples and to teach them to obey all that he had commanded (*Matt.* 28:20). Paul was faithful to both aspects of that commission.

He describes their new life as one that aims to please God. In this way Paul captures the very essence of the Christian life.

(i) It is first of all a life governed by a relationship rather than by rules. The gospel reconciles us to God and creates a vital personal relationship with him. Our new life is lived out of the context of this wonderful relationship. It can never be allowed to degenerate into the heartless performance of duties and dull adherence to conventions. These are soul-less substitutes for the real thing.

(ii) Specifically, it is a life bent on pleasing God. While we can never merit God's favour, we can live in ways that please him. We do that by knowing and doing his will (*Rom.* 12:2, *Eph.* 5:10). This has always been the way to please him and walk worthy of his calling. Israel was to respond to God's redeeming grace by keeping the commandments given to them at Mount Sinai (*Exod.* 19:5–6). Similarly, Paul prayed that the Colossians would be filled with the knowledge of God's will in order that they may 'live a life worthy of the Lord and may please him in every way' (*Col.* 1:9–10).

Christian living aims to do the revealed will of God. But it does so in order to please, never to earn. Obedience is never a supplement to God's grace, but it is always the fitting response to it.

PROGRESS IN THE CHRISTIAN LIFE

The Thessalonian Christians had made a start in this new way of life. Paul is quick to encourage his readers by acknowledging that. He knows how easy it is to dishearten young believers by harping on faults and weaknesses. Before turning to these, as he knows he must, he makes a point of affirming the progress they have made already.

But while glad about this, he is not content – and does not want them to be, either. There is still plenty of room for progress. There-fore, he asks and urges them in the Lord Jesus to do this more and more (v.1).

It may well be that Paul is simply repeating himself when he both asks and urges his readers to make further progress in the life that pleases God. But the two expressions may reflect two different tones in his appeal. His 'asking' them might be the affectionate request of a friend, and his 'urging' them the more authoritative demand of an apostle. This blending of affection and authority lies at the heart of pastoral effectiveness. It is winsome on the one hand, but has bite on the other.

We must note, too, that this appeal is made in the Lord Jesus (v.1). It really comes not from Paul, but from the Lord through him. And it also comes to those who through faith are themselves now 'in the Lord Jesus'. It belongs to their new life in him to grow more and more. The Christian life is one of constant and gradual growth in

God-pleasing obedience. We shall never be able to say we have reached the mark until we are finally with Christ and like him (*Phil.* 3:12–14).

AUTHORITY AND THE CHRISTIAN LIFE

This appeal is reinforced by a reminder that the original instructions the Thessalonians had received had been by the authority of the Lord Jesus (v.2). Paul is not bluffing or misusing the name of the Lord in encouraging further progress. Spiritual growth is undoubtedly his will, because the original instructions were his.

This was something they already knew well. Paul's preaching in Thessalonica had been attended with such spiritual power (1:5) that his hearers had accepted his message as the word of God rather than of man (2:13). His apostolic credentials had never come into question. His hearers had appreciated that the source of his gospel and his instructions lay in Christ himself.

In fact, Paul heightens the idea that he was merely acting as the Lord's messenger. He passed on instructions (v.2) in the same way that a military courier passes on orders from a superior officer. His words had the full authority of the Lord Jesus behind them.

This note of authority is worth pondering. The God-pleasing life is not presented to us as a lofty ideal worth aspiring to. It comes to us as a demand backed by the full authority of the Lord Jesus Christ our King. Cold obedience out of duty will never satisfy him. But neither will an ambivalent take-it-or-leave-it attitude. He positively requires that we devote ourselves gladly and gratefully to a life that pleases God.

15

Called to a Holy Life

³It is God's will that you should be sanctified: that you should avoid sexual immorality; ⁴that each of you should learn to control his own body in a way that is holy and honourable, ⁵not in passionate lust like the heathen, who do not know God; ⁶and that in this matter no-one should wrong his brother or take advantage of him. The Lord will punish men for all such sins, as we have already told you and warned you. ⁷For God did not call us to be impure, but to live a holy life. ⁸Therefore, he who rejects this instruction does not reject man but God, who gives you his Holy Spirit (1 Thess. 4:3–8).

P aul wanted to see his converts in Thessalonica more firmly established in the faith. They had made a good start, but there was still plenty of room for improvement and progress (3:10; 4:1). This was particularly true in the area of practical Christian living. Paul's gospel had not only summoned them to believe in the true God and his Son, but it had called them to live in a way that was pleasing to him. Coming as many of them did from a pagan background, this meant making massive adjustments.

Three issues of practical living are singled out for special treatment in these and the following verses: sexual purity (vv.3–8), brotherly love (vv.9–10), and daily life in the world (vv.11–12).

SANCTIFICATION

The apostle's relentless concern to see his converts make progress in the Christian life was no quirk of personal character. He could ask and urge the Thessalonians to press on to greater levels of obedience (v.1) because it was God's will that they should be sanctified (v.3). It was not Paul the perfectionist who was demanding 'more and more', but the pure and holy God who had called them. Paul wanted believers to be sanctified 'through and through' (5:23) because he knew that God had from the beginning chosen them to be saved through the Spirit's sanctifying work (*2 Thess.* 2:13). Correspondingly, he made it his goal to present the Gentiles 'an offering acceptable to God, sanctified by the Holy Spirit' (*Rom.* 15:16).

Sanctification, in this context, is the process of people becoming holy. Sometimes the term is used in a more objective sense to refer to the state of believers through their union with Christ (*1 Cor.* 1:2, 30). Through faith in him we are set apart to God and become saints (*Rom.* 1:7). But in addition to that, there is also a subjective or inner work of transformation within us that God accomplishes through his Spirit. Gradually and progressively we are freed from all that defiles and transformed into the image of Jesus (*2 Cor.* 3:18).

Sanctification in this sense is the process that leads to holiness. Every Christian experiences this all-too-often painful makeover because it is God's purpose to change us into his own likeness. Christianity without transformation is unknown. Without holiness, no one shall see the Lord (*Heb.* 12:14).

SEXUAL PURITY

Having stated God's purpose, Paul adds immediately the specific application that the Thessalonians are to avoid sexual immorality (v.3). This is not to say that sanctification is limited to achieving sexual purity, but it does mean that God's transforming grace must be at work in this specific area.

It would not have surprised Paul's readers that sexual purity should feature so prominently in a discussion on sanctification. They lived in a culture famous for its sexual permissiveness. Every form of sexual vice was rampant in the Greco-Roman world of the first century, and its expression had freest rein in major port cities like Thessalonica. More than likely, many of the church members in that city had themselves been caught up in immoral relationships before conversion. If so, they may well have continued to feel the imperious tug of sexual attraction for past partners.

Paul, aware of this and perhaps conscious that there were members of the church with a decided weakness in this area (5:14), insists that they should avoid sexual immorality. He deliberately uses a broad or inclusive term, the Greek word *porneia*, to indicate that he has in view a range of sexual aberrations. He urges an absolute break with such practices. The Christian life is to be marked by both radical restraint and purity in the sexual realm.

This idea of restraint is taken up further in a second directive. It is God's will that each should learn to control his own body in a way that is holy and honourable (v.4). Bible students have long held different views on what these words are actually saying.

(i) The translation we are following suggests that they refer to the control of our natural sexual urges. Others contend, however, that they are saying that sexual desires are to be fulfilled within marriage, and that in a restrained and honourable way.

(ii) The two interpretations hinge on how the words 'control' (*ktaomai*) and 'body' (*skeuos*) are understood. The former is more commonly translated 'acquire' or 'possess' (*Luke* 21:19, *Acts* 8:20), and the latter 'vessel' (*Acts* 9:15), sometimes understood in the sense of 'wife' (*1 Pet.* 3:7). This leads to the alternate translations in the NIV margin, 'learn to live with his own wife' or 'learn to acquire a wife'.

Whichever the precise meaning intended, the general message is clear. Christians are to curb their natural sexual instincts and express them in a way that is holy and honourable. They are not to live in passionate lust, gripped and borne along by their desires. They are to differ from their pagan neighbours and not share the lifestyle of those who do not know God (v.5). God abandons those who reject him to the tyranny of their corrupt passions (*Rom.* 1:24–27). But as those who now know the Lord, believers are to live holy and self-controlled lives, especially in the realm of their sexual relationships.

Paul has one more word on this subject. He recognises that immorality affects other people as well as the principal offenders. A wife suffers when a husband is unfaithful, a prospective husband is robbed when his future wife's purity is stained, and the marriage bed is horribly defiled when same-sex perversions are practised.

Knowing that sexual immorality is always a breach of love, Paul insists that in this matter no one should wrong his brother or take advantage of him (v.6).

Adultery is probably the vice that is foremost in his mind when he mentions this. He recognises that it is still a threat within the Christian community in Thessalonica. Like a fraud in the world of commerce, an adulterer invades the rights of others and plunders what is not lawfully his. This must not happen among Christians.

MOTIVES FOR PURITY

The apostle reinforces these frank and strong directions with a stern warning. He reminds his readers that the sexually immoral will face God's judgement (v.6), a truth his readers already knew, for he had already warned them about this while with them. The reality of a final judgement was part of Paul's gospel preaching (*Rom*. 2:16, *Acts* 17:31), and the culpability of the sexually immoral at that judgement was a point of special focus. He insisted that such people would not enter the kingdom of God (*1 Cor*. 1:9, *Eph*. 5:5) and that God's wrath comes on those who are disobedient (*Eph*. 5:6).

But the threat of future judgement was not the only reason the Thessalonian Christians needed to avoid all forms of sexual immorality. God's purpose for them as his people was an added motive to purity. He had not called them to be impure, but to live a holy life (v.7). God's choice and call was to shape the way they lived. He intended them to be his special possession, a people sharing his own holiness (*Heb*. 12:10, *1 Pet*. 1:16). How could they – or their counterparts in any age – abandon themselves to immorality when they had such a destiny?

AN INESCAPABLE DEMAND

Perhaps some members in the church were contesting Paul's earlier teaching on this subject. If so, it is these people in particular whom he addresses when he adds that those who reject this instruction reject not man but God (v.8). He has said enough about God's will for their sanctification to make it irrefutably clear that sexual purity is not merely a human ideal but a divine demand. To contend otherwise, or to insist that acts of the body are indifferent, was to reject not only Paul's instructions but also the God who was behind them. More than that, it was to fly in the face of his most gracious gift, the Holy Spirit, given for the very purpose of making them holy. To spurn God's demand cannot but grieve his Spirit.

These instructions on sex ethics speak just as urgently to our generation as they did to Paul's first readers. As our culture slides ever increasingly into moral decadence, Christians need to remember that as God's holy people (*Eph.* 5:3), they must aim at absolute sexual purity.

16

Brotherly Love

⁹Now about brotherly love we do not need to write to you, for you yourselves have been taught by God to love each other. ¹⁰And in fact, you do love all the brothers throughout Macedonia. Yet we urge you, brothers, to do so more and more (1 Thess. 4:9–10).

Two qualities made early Christians stand out from their pagan neighbours. One was their moral purity, the other their intense love for one another.

Having written about the first of these (4:3–8), nothing could be more natural for the apostle than to turn to the second (vv.9–10). But whereas his discussion of sexual purity has an urgency about it that suggests problems facing the church in this area, his comments on love are brief and bright with commendation. His readers were not lacking in love. Indeed, the evidence of this virtue in the church had already given Paul reason for praise and thanks (1:3; 3:6).

NATURE

The love Paul has in mind is specifically brotherly love (v.9), the love of Christians for one another. The term is a translation of the Greek word *philadelphia*, a word originally used to describe the special affection family members felt for one another. Christians, recognising that they had been born into a great spiritual family, soon applied it to the love they felt for one another. The same instinctive affection they felt toward their natural brothers and sisters they found they now shared with all their fellow Christians.

Brotherly love differs somewhat from the love (*agape*) Jesus commanded his followers to show to each other and all men (*John* 13:34). *Agape* is a love that does not depend on the nature of the relationship between people. It is a steady, selfless, self-giving attitude born out of a genuine concern for others irrespective of who they are or what condition they are in. It is the love God showed us when we were still sinners (*Rom.* 5:8) and the love we are to show our enemies (*Matt.* 5:44). Of course, we are to show this self-denying love toward each other as Christians. But as we do so in the context of our new family relationship, this love takes on a quality of closeness, affection and mutuality that makes it proper to call it 'brotherly love'.

SOURCE

Paul says that he has no need to write to the Thessalonians about this subject; they have been taught by God to love each other (v.9).

He probably means that the Holy Spirit living in their hearts (v.8) had taught them to love one another. True, there were other senses in which it might be said that God had taught them to love. He had revealed the duty to love through the Old Testament Scriptures (*Lev.* 19:18), and that had been passed on to them through the teaching and tradition of Christ (*1 Thess.* 4:2). Perhaps he had even given special prophetic revelations (5:20) instructing the church in this duty. These are all possible ways in which it could be said that God had taught them. But none of them capture the intimacy and effectiveness of the teaching implied in these words.

The Thessalonians had not simply been taught *about* the subject of brotherly love; God himself had actually taught them *to* love. This suggests that God had been at work within them, as Jeremiah had predicted, to write his law on their hearts (*Jer.* 31:33). The Holy Spirit is his agent in this work. He produces the fruit of love when he takes up residence in our hearts (*Gal.* 5:22). Love is actually bred into us, making it evident that we are born of God and that we truly belong to him (*1 John* 4:7).

The same can be said in fact for every spiritual quality we possess. Sinful human nature cannot love, or be patient, self-controlled, forgiving, or generous to those in need (*Gal.* 5:19ff., *Rom.* 7:18). God has to teach us do these things through his Spirit. He uses means such as his Word, prayer, the sacraments, Christian fellowship and ministry to do so, but it is nevertheless the Spirit alone who makes these means effective in our lives. All true believers can say they have been taught by God (*John* 6:45), and they must look to God to carry on the work of transformation that he has begun.

SCOPE

The brotherly love of the Thessalonian Christians showed itself not only among themselves, but toward other Christians as well. Almost with a note of glad surprise, Paul remarks that they had not simply been taught to love, but that they in fact do love all the brothers throughout Macedonia (v.10).

Located as they were in the principal city of Macedonia, the believers in Thessalonica would have often had contact with Christians from other towns and cities in the region. Merchants, farmers and traders would have visited the city regularly, and the Christians among them would naturally have sought the hospitality of their brothers and sisters in Christ (*Titus* 3:14). In this way the church there would have come to know of the whereabouts of other groups of Christians in the province and been kept up to date with their welfare. Members of the city church may also have gone out on preaching tours in surrounding towns (1:8) and may themselves have journeyed to Philippi or Berea for business or other purposes. By these and various other means a warm spirit of love had developed toward all the brothers in Macedonia.

This broad-hearted love for fellow Christians was a mark of the early church. Paul thanked God for its presence in the Ephesian Christians (*Eph.* 1:15), in the Colossians (*Col.* 1:4), and in the slave owner Philemon (*Philem.* 5). God's love formed in the heart is a love that reaches out and embraces all who are his children. To use the Apostle John's words, 'Everyone who loves the Father loves his child as well' (*1 John* 5:1).

Sadly, this spirit is not always present among us today. Denominationalism, painful doctrinal differences, unresolved personal tensions, and the sheer individualism of our culture have created suspicion and aloofness where affection ought to reign. Recapturing a warm spirit of Christian kinship among all true believers is a challenge that has faced the church in every age. It surely remains a priority in our own.

GROWTH

As genuine as the love of his readers was for each other, Paul was not satisfied. In one breath he praises them for loving one another, and in the next he urges them to do so more and more (v.10).

As we have seen more than once already, in making such a demand Paul is not just being hard to please. He knows that no matter how much progress has been made in the Christian life, much more can always be made. So abundant is the new life we have in Christ that we can never contain or exhaust its fullness. Paul can speak of the 'unsearchable riches of Christ' (*Eph*. 3:8) and of his love that 'surpasses knowledge' (*Eph*. 3:19). The measure of knowledge or love that we possess now is only a fragment of the vast fullness there is to know.

Brotherly love, for example, may grow in a number of directions. It may grow in breadth as it reaches out to embrace more of our fellow Christians. It may grow in depth as it enters more deeply into the hurts and joys of others. And it may grow in length as it forbears more patiently and forgives more heartily. A commitment to love others well will call us to grow more and more in this grace.

No Christian can ever say that they love to the limits. At best we all paddle in the shallows, experiencing little and expressing still less of the boundless ocean of God's love. He calls us and longs for us to wade out into the depths.

17

Practical Daily Living

[11]Make it your ambition to lead a quiet life, to mind your own business and to work with your hands, just as we told you, [12]so that your daily life may win the respect of outsiders and so that you will not be dependent on anybody (1 Thess. 4:11–12).

The congregation in Thessalonica seems to have been burdened with a class of people best described as idlers (5:14). They were probably church members overexcited about the second coming of Jesus. Believing this to be very close at hand, they had stopped working and now lived in a state of idle dependence and agitated anticipation. In their misguided enthusiasm they became a nuisance and a burden to the Christian community. They had also brought it into disrepute in the eyes of the watching pagan world.

Having just spoken about Christian love in the church (vv.9–10), Paul turns to deal with this new problem. It may well be that he considered the two matters closely related. Brotherly love in the church had generated a liberality and kindness that loafers were ready to abuse. Paul wants to make it clear that true Christianity expresses itself in a quiet and industrious manner of daily life.

A QUIET LIFE

Addressing the congregation as a whole, the apostle stresses the importance of leading a quiet life (v.11). This command has the appearance of self-contradiction. The word translated 'ambition' literally means 'to strive for, to press after wholeheartedly'. It is an energetic word. Paul, in effect, is telling his readers to strive energetically to be 'quiet', a remarkable paradox.

The quietness he has in mind, however, is not lethargic passivity. Put simply, he is not saying that Christians are to strive to be lazy! When he speaks of a quiet life, he means a steady and sober life, the kind of life that contrasts with the fervid, restless excitement associated with overheated minds.

He seems to be addressing the problem mentioned above created by a misapplication of the promise of the Lord Jesus' second coming. Excitement bordering on fanaticism had created a noisy and disturbing restlessness among some church members. They could not settle and had become totally unproductive members both of society and of the Christian church. The quietness Paul commends is the complete opposite of this condition. He wants believers to wait eagerly for the coming of the Lord Jesus, but to do so in a sober and steady manner rather than in a condition of unsettled distraction (*1 Pet.* 4:7).

Closely connected with this is the instruction to mind their own business (v.11). People gripped by novel or unbalanced notions generally cannot confine their convictions to themselves. Their restlessness drives them to invade the privacy of others, often in an arrogant and strident manner.

The same peril threatens when people are inactive through idleness. They are inclined to become busybodies, venturing uninvited into the affairs of others, creating hurt and disruption wherever they go (*1 Tim.* 5:13). It was this plague that Paul wanted to see rooted out of the church in Thessalonica. We must continue to be on guard against it today.

AN INDUSTRIOUS LIFE

The antidote to a meddlesome and restless life is one of diligent labour. Paul wants his readers to make it their ambition to work with their own hands (v.11).

It would appear, especially from the fuller record in the second letter to the church (*2 Thess.* 3:6–10), that some of the congregation had abandoned their daily work. They probably thought that since the return of the Lord Jesus was so near there was really no need to provide for the future. Indeed, they may have thought that to work was to show a lack of faith.

It may be, however, that some were simply sponging on the liberality of others. The promise of the Lord's return gave them a reason for being lazy, and the kindness of the new community made it possible for them to live without working.

Whatever lay behind the problem, Paul does not condone it for a moment. The most fervent expectation of the Lord's return is no reason to abandon daily responsibilities. The best way to prepare for the coming of Christ is to be faithful in the work he has given us to do (*Matt.* 24:45–51). For many of Paul's readers, that meant busying themselves with the work of their hands. In encouraging this, Paul is probably urging his readers to some form of productive manual labour. He himself engaged in tent-making to provide for his own and his helpers' needs (2:9, *Acts* 20:34).

Interestingly, cultured Greeks despised work of this kind and owned slaves or employed labourers to avoid doing it themselves. Christianity clashed with popular culture at that point. It dignified manual labour as an essential part of God's purpose for man. Here Paul also advocates it as a means of self-support.

A RESPECTABLE LIFE

The apostle gives two reasons for pressing for this kind of lifestyle. The first is that their daily life might win the respect of outsiders (v.12).

Paul knew well, of course, that Christians could never please their unbelieving neighbours in every respect. The world would never accept Christ's followers as its own (*John* 15:21; *1 John* 3:1). To court acceptance could only be at the cost of compromising their new life in Christ.

That understood, however, Paul was insistent that believers should live in a way that wins the respect of the watching world. The gospel does not disrupt lawful occupations and social relationships. It makes people better citizens and neighbours, better parents and relatives. Unbelievers should be able to look at the way Christians work and live and go away respecting them deeply (*1 Pet.* 2:12). More than that, they should be convinced that the gospel makes people more – rather than less – responsible in the practical affairs of life.

It is this relationship between daily life and the gospel that lies behind Paul's instructions here. He wants Christians to live in a way that breeds respect, not scorn (*Titus* 2:10). Lazy, fanatical, meddlesome Christians create a stumbling block to conversion. Quiet and diligent lives can make the most degraded pagan look twice at a Christian and his gospel.

AN INDEPENDENT LIFE

The second reason offered for living a quiet and industrious lifestyle is so that they would not be dependent upon anybody (v.12).

In one respect, the Christian gospel does encourage people to be dependent upon others. Within the body of Christ we need to rely on one another, and we must learn to receive from others as well as give to them (*1 Cor.* 12:14–26). From this point of view, self-sufficiency is a sin.

But Paul is not thinking of this kind of mutual dependence here. He is referring to dependence upon others for food and clothing and other daily necessities. Those refusing to work had become parasites on their hard-working but generous neighbours. This was not only a bad witness to the world, it was a burden to the church. It was creating unnecessary stress and perhaps preventing others who needed help from being helped. Communal love within the church calls for people to work hard to provide for their own needs and to have extra to help the indigent and needy (*Eph.* 4:28). Paul's dictum was 'if a man will not work, he shall not eat' (*2 Thess.* 3:10).

It scarcely needs to be mentioned in closing that the problem of idleness addressed in this passage is not the same as the inactivity resulting from unemployment or disability. One is the result of sloth and self-deception; the other is the outcome of economic or health factors beyond a person's control. The former is cause for shame, the latter calls for understanding and support.

18

Not Without Hope

¹³Brothers, we do not want you to be ignorant about those who fall asleep, or to grieve like the rest of men, who have no hope. ¹⁴We believe that Jesus died and rose again and so we believe that God will bring with Jesus those who have fallen asleep in him (1 Thess. 4:13–14).

A new topic comes into focus in these and the following verses. From this point to 5:11, Paul is absorbed with explaining more about the second coming of the Jesus.

The idea of the personal return of the Lord Jesus had clearly been central to the gospel preached in Thessalonica. We have already encountered reference to it several times in this letter (1:10; 2:19; 3:13), and in each instance it is raised in a way that assumes the readers know about it. Paul is writing not to acquaint the Thessalonians with this event, but to clear up difficulties concerning it that had arisen in the months since he had left them.

Two difficulties were troubling at least some in the church. The first (4:13–18) was the fate of Christians who die before Jesus comes back. Would they miss out on being part of that event, or at least be disadvantaged in some way?

Secondly (5:1–11), apparently some were anxious about the timing of the Lord's return. They knew that he would come suddenly and that the exact time of his return was something God had not revealed (5:1). But would they be ready for him? What if he were to come back when they were not expecting him? Would they be losers because of this?

To allay unnecessary fears on these two points, Paul explains more about the second coming.

UNHELPFUL IGNORANCE

In addressing the first of these problems, he begins by saying, 'We do not want you to be ignorant' (v.13). In using this common formula (cf. *Rom.* 11:25, *1 Cor.* 10:1; 12:1), Paul pinpoints the root of their anxieties. He traces them to a lack of knowledge, to ignorance.

As stated above, the missionaries had introduced the Thessalonians to the idea that Jesus the Messiah would return again as God's triumphant king. But just how much they had told them about this event is unclear. We can safely assume that they passed on such basic facts as its suddenness and glory, and that it would signal the end of this age. They probably taught them other things as well.

However, it is one thing to understand facts such as these, but another to work out their implications for practical life. It was at this point that anxiety reared its head. The believers needed to know more.

Ignorance is often the cause of anxiety among Christians. A simple understanding of the gospel may be enough to lead us to saving faith in Christ. But it is seldom enough to equip us to live faith-filled lives in a world of suffering. We need to leave the elementary teachings and go on to maturity (*Heb.* 6:1). Not a few doubts and timid fears are traceable to a failure to grow in knowledge.

Specifically, the Thessalonian Christians needed to know more about those who had 'fallen asleep', that is, those who had died (v.13). Sleep was a term used widely in the ancient world for death. Among pagans it was a euphemism to soften the dread that death inspired. But among Christians it was a fitting expression of the hope they cherished. To the believer, death was like falling asleep at the end of a long period of toil (*Rev.* 14:13) in the anticipation of awakening refreshed on a new day.

From what we can gather, the Thessalonians were worried about what would happen to dead Christians when Jesus returned. Their future hopes were very much focused on this great event. They knew that Jesus would return in kingly power to usher in a new order of things. Would their dead brothers and sisters miss out on this event and its accompanying blessings? This thought had not occurred to them while Paul was with them, but now that perhaps some of their own fellowship had died, it had become an issue of great importance.

UNWARRANTED GRIEF

Before taking up this matter, Paul tells why he is so eager to see their minds put at rest about it. He does not want them to grieve like others who have no hope (v.13).

Death was a prospect people dreaded in Paul's day, even as they do in our own. While some Greek philosophers taught that the soul was immortal and that it was released at death from the prison-house of its body, death nevertheless remained a frightening unknown to most people. For them the netherworld was a shadowy and chilly realm to be feared. Only the living had hope. There was no hope in death. Consequently, the grief of pagans was often marked by despair. No ray of hope relieved their sorrow.

It is this kind of grief that Paul wants his readers to avoid. He is not saying that they cannot express sorrow when friends and relatives die, even deep, heart-numbing sorrow. Grief itself, even intense grief, is not the point at issue. What is at stake is grief without hope. Christians should never sorrow without a strong underlying assurance of the good things to come promised in the gospel. Christians can and should grieve, but it is always sub-Christian to grieve without hope.

UNBREAKABLE UNION

How then does Paul deal with the issue of believers who die before the second coming? He does so firstly in the form of a logical de- duction (v.14). The death and resurrection of Jesus is the starting point of his argument. The twin facts that Jesus both died and rose again were foundational truths of the gospel that both Paul and his readers believed. They received them by faith as historical certainties.

Now, the apostle continues, just as we believe Jesus to have died and risen again, so we believe that God will bring with Jesus those who have died in him. Certainty about the second reality is grounded in the certainty of the first.

Two things about this second part of Paul's statement need to be noted.

(i) The first is the new object of faith to which it refers. It is not, as we might expect, the fact that believers, too, shall rise again, just as Jesus did. Rather, it is that when the Lord Jesus returns, God will bring with him those who have already died and gone to be with him (cf. 3:13). True, they will return still as disembodied spirits, but the vital thing is that they will not miss out on the presence or coming of the king (the *parousia*), as some evidently feared they would.

(ii) Secondly, note who it is that God will bring with Jesus at his coming: those who sleep in Jesus. They are people who have died, but who even in death are still in Jesus. Death does not dissolve the bond between a believer and the Lord. It merely ushers them into his more immediate presence in glory (*Phil.* 1:23), where they wait with him for the end of this present age and the final appearance of God's righteous kingdom (2:12).

How does Paul connect these two grand objects of faith – the death and resurrection of Jesus, and the coming of the dead in Christ with him at his triumphant return? Evidently he holds the death and resurrection of Christ as both the pattern and guarantee of what lies ahead for all who believe in him and who are consequently united to him through faith. Did Jesus die and then rise again in bodily form from the grave to live to God? Then all who are in him, though they die, will also share in the experience of bodily resurrection (*Rom.* 6:5). And when will that happen? It will happen when Jesus returns, just as he himself said it would (*John* 5:28–29). That being so, the dead in Christ must return with him at his coming so that they, too, can share in the glorious event of resurrection.

Paul has more to say on this in the following verses. For the moment we must simply note his pastoral method. The anxiety of his readers was related to their lack of knowledge and spiritual insight. Its relief lies in a deeper understanding of Christ and the significance of his death and resurrection.

We, too, shall find over and over again that our spiritual fears and uncertainties stem from a failure to understand all that God has accomplished in Christ for us. A deeper appreciation of the gospel holds the remedy to a multitude of our perplexities.

19

Definitely Not Left Out!

15According to the Lord's own word, we tell you that we who are still alive, who are left till the coming of the Lord, will certainly not precede those who have fallen asleep. 16For the Lord himself will come down from heaven, with a loud command, with the voice of the archangel and with the trumpet call of God, and the dead in Christ will rise first. 17After that, we who are still alive and are left will be caught up together with them in the clouds to meet the Lord in the air. And so we will be with the Lord forever. 18Therefore encourage each other with these words (1 Thess. 4:15–18).

Paul wants to assure anxious Christians that those who die in the Lord will not be left out of the events that take place when the Lord Jesus returns. He has already shown how the death and resurrection of Jesus guarantee that they will be with him when he comes again. Now he goes on to describe what will actually happen to living and dead believers at that time.

In doing so he provides the fullest description of the *parousia* or coming of the Lord that we have in the New Testament. It must be realised, however, that Paul is not attempting to tell us everything that will take place at that time. For example, he says nothing at all about what will happen to non-Christians when Jesus returns. This is not, as some suggest, because they do not come into the picture until a further, later coming of the Lord to earth. Rather, they are not mentioned because they are not relevant to the specific pastoral issue Paul is addressing – the participation of those who have died in the coming *parousia*. To use what he says here as a starting point for speculation is unhelpful and distorts his intention.

NO ADVANTAGE

The essence of what Paul wants to say is that those who are still alive will not precede those who have died (v.15). Though it will indeed be a wonderful thing to be alive when the Lord comes back, those who have died will not be left behind or in any way be disadvantaged.

Paul's authority for saying this rests on the Lord's own word (v.15). He does not attempt to calm his readers with his own opinion or logic, and still less with wishful thinking. There can be no surer foundation for comfort than the teaching of the Lord Jesus himself. His word puts an end to all doubt.

But which word does Paul have in mind here? Is he referring to one of Jesus' statements recorded in the Gospels? This is unlikely, since none provide an exact match to what the apostle is about to tell us here. He is more probably referring to an unrecorded saying of the Lord that became part of the oral tradition of the early church, or perhaps to some special prophetic revelation that either he or someone else had received. Whatever the source, Paul has a word of the Lord upon which to base his encouragement.

THE DEAD RAISED FIRST

That word assures us that when Jesus returns, the first thing that will happen to believers is that the dead in Christ will rise (v.16). Paul gives a vivid account of the two events leading up to that.

(i) The Lord himself will come down from heaven (v.16). After his resurrection the Lord Jesus Christ ascended to sit at the right hand of God in heaven. He will return to earth from there, descending in the same way that his disciples saw him leave (*Acts* 1:11). His coming will be personal (it will be the Lord himself who comes), bodily, and visible.

(ii) His descent will be marked by mighty sounds. Three sounds are mentioned – a loud command, the voice of the archangel and the trumpet call of God (v.16). Whether these are three distinct noises or are simply different ways of saying the same thing is debated. But it is plain that the three expressions all refer to an authoritative and irresistible summons. They all have a ring of authority and note of urgency about them. The command resembles the cry of a charioteer to his horses, the archangel is the powerful messenger of God, and the trumpet is an instrument of summons and celebration. The Lord returns as a conquering king and announces his coming with a mighty sound.

Next the dead in Christ rise. Paul emphasises that this is the first thing that will happen. There will be living believers on earth, but before anything happens to them, the bodies of the dead will rise at the sound of the Lord's voice (*John* 5:28). Just how these bodies will be reconstituted and reunited with their spirits is not mentioned, and it is pointless for us to speculate about something so obviously supernatural. The point Paul establishes is that those who have died are active participants in the events of this great moment in history. At least momentarily they co-exist on earth in bodily form with the living (whose bodies are also transformed 'in the twinkling of an eye', *1 Cor.* 15:52) before the next stage in the drama unfolds.

RAPTURE AND REUNION

Following the resurrection of the dead, we who are still alive will be caught up together with them in the clouds to meet the Lord in the air (v.17).

This spectacular event is what has come to be known in Christian theology as the rapture. The word 'rapture' comes from a Latin term meaning 'to seize'. It aptly conveys the ideas of force, suddenness and irresistibility implied in the original verb Paul used. Believers, both the transformed living and the resurrected dead, will be snatched up from the earth to meet with the Lord in the air.

This meeting with the Lord is the high point of the *parousia* as Paul describes it here. It is a personal reunion or gathering together of the Lord with his redeemed saints in their glorified bodies. At last he sees his saving work for them in full fruition. The heavenly groom welcomes his bride into his immediate presence forever.

Fittingly, this takes place in the clouds in the air (v.17). Clouds are symbols of God's presence and serve as his royal chariot (*Psa.* 104:3). Before descending completely to earth, then, the divine Lord calls his people to meet with him in the air. They are to be identified with him in all that follows, even in the judgement of angels and of the world. Appropriately then, they meet him as he comes down from heaven, both to welcome him, and to join him.

When speaking of believers meeting with the Lord in the air, Paul may indeed have more than a mere reunion in view. The term he uses to describe that reunion (*apantesis*) was used in the ancient world to refer to the official welcome offered to a king or other high dignitary when he visited a city. The leading officials of the city would go some distance outside its walls to meet their visitor before escorting him in to conduct his business. It may well be that for Paul, the reunion of believers with Jesus in the air forms the prelude to his coming to judge the world.

SURE GROUNDS FOR COMFORT

If the troubled believers in Thessalonica would keep these things before them, their fears concerning the future of dead Christians would evaporate. The Lord's words make it clear that the dead in Christ will not be upstaged by the living at the *parousia*, but join with them fully in all that great event entails.

Paul tells his readers to encourage each other with these words (v.18). Christian comfort is grounded in more than sympathy. It is based upon the hope conveyed by truth. The very best thing we can do to comfort the grieving is to share with them, at the right time and in the right way, the promises contained in the gospel.

Paul's words in this passage challenge us deeply today. Do we share the same eager anticipation of the *parousia* that marked the early church? Does the prospect of meeting the Lord thrill us as it ought to? Are we able to echo from the heart the cry of the Spirit and the bride, 'Come!' (*Rev.* 22:17)?

20

Like a Thief in the Night

¹Now, brothers, about times and dates we do not need to write to you, ²for you know very well that the day of the Lord will come like a thief in the night. ³While people are saying, 'Peace and safety,' destruction will come on them suddenly, as labour pains on a pregnant woman, and they will not escape (1 Thess. 5:1–3).

Having dealt with anxieties about the dead in Christ, Paul moves on to a new but closely related subject. His teaching on the coming of the Lord had aroused fears in the minds of some as to whether they would be ready for this great event. This in turn had prompted them to ask about its timing. They wanted to ensure that they would be ready for it and not miss out on their salvation.

UNNECESSARY INFORMATION

Their query concerned times and dates relating to the coming day of the Lord. They wanted to know precisely when the Lord would come, and perhaps, too, the events that would characterise the times of his appearing. A fascination with knowing these details continues to grip many today.

As noted above, their reason for wanting this information was intensely practical. They knew that Jesus' return would be an awesome event, and they wanted to be better prepared for it. Their mistake lay in supposing that the best way to be ready for his coming was to know its exact time.

Concerning this, Paul says that he really has no need to write because, in effect, he has no new information to give. Earlier we noted that he saw no need to write about the subject of brotherly love (4:9). That was because the church had been taught by God himself to love. But here he sees no need to write because his readers already know very well all they need to know on the subject. Paul and his helpers had obviously made it very clear while with them that the precise timing of Jesus' return was something that only the Father knew (*Matt.* 24:36). Their present knowledge was accurate and totally sufficient for their needs.

UNKNOWN TIMING

He had taught them enough to know that the day of the Lord would come like a thief in the night (v.2). The thief metaphor was one Jesus himself had used when teaching his disciples about his coming (*Luke* 12:39). It naturally suggests unexpectedness, surprise, alarm and devastation. A thief does not forewarn a victim of his visit, usually catches them unprepared, and invariably comes to spoil rather than reward. All of these thoughts are probably intended in its use in this context. The day of the Lord will come upon people suddenly, unexpectedly and with devastating effect.

This latter idea of devastation is closely related to the term Paul uses here to refer to the return of the Lord. He does not speak of the *parousia*, the presence or coming of the Lord, but of 'the day of the Lord'. This expression has its roots in the Old Testament (*Amos* 5:18, *Isa.* 13:6–16, *Joel* 1:15). It commonly applies to God breaking into history to judge his enemies and save his people. The day of the Lord is characteristically a day of wrath and destruction for rebellious individuals and nations, and at the same time a day of salvation and deliverance for his people.

In the New Testament, the day of the Lord is intimately connected with the coming of the Lord Jesus. In his second letter to the Thessalonians, Paul actually identifies the day of the Lord with the *parousia* (*2 Thess.* 2:1ff.). He sees the two as different aspects of a single event. The coming of the Lord Jesus for his people (4:13–18) will also be his coming to judge the world, to end this present order, and to usher in the eternal state. For those who have not believed the gospel, the day of the Lord will be one of fierce wrath and terror. But for believers, it will be a day of joy and reunion (*2 Thess.* 1:9–10).

UNSUSPECTED ARRIVAL

It is the former class of people – unbelievers – Paul has in mind as he continues (v.3). He is thinking of mankind in general, not of believers like the Thessalonian Christians. The state of the mass of mankind at the coming of the Lord will be one of unsuspecting tranquillity. Jesus told his disciples that at his return conditions would be just as they were in Noah's day before the flood. People will be eating and drinking, marrying and giving in marriage (*Matt.* 24:38), just as though everything was always going to carry on as it always had (*2 Pet.* 3:4).

According to Paul, people will be saying 'Peace and safety' at that time. Far from anticipating a divine visitation, they will be basking in inward calm and outward security. Their state will mirror the complacency of apostate Judah before the Babylonian exile. Lulled by lying prophets into thinking all was well, the people of that time lived as though the warnings of Jeremiah and other prophets were an idle tale (*Jer.* 6:14; 8:11, *Ezek.* 13:10). Little did they realise the calamity hovering overhead.

This, of course, is the state of increasing numbers in our day. As secularism chokes out any belief in an avenging God, and as the church shies away from declaring the certainty of future judgement, the thought of a final day of reckoning fades increasingly from the consciousness of men and women. As unpopular as it may be to do so, the certainty of the day of the Lord needs to be heralded urgently and clearly to awaken our unsuspecting generation.

INESCAPABLE DESTRUCTION

This is particularly so in view of the sudden and inescapable judgement that will come upon people in that day (v.3). Destruction will be the fate of the unprepared in the day of the Lord. The term does not suggest obliteration or annihilation, as some contend. Rooted in Old Testament images of God's historical judgements, it points to the overwhelming of men and women with suffering, death and loss. When God destroys his enemies he brings about their complete ruin, the utter loss of all that makes life worthwhile. In his second letter to the Thessalonian church, Paul will speak of unbelievers being punished with 'everlasting destruction and shut out from the presence of the Lord and the majesty of his power' (*2 Thess.* 1:9). This is the fate he has in mind here.

The apostle uses another image, the birth pangs of a pregnant woman. Elsewhere it is used in the Bible to express the pain and agony of an unpleasant experience (*Psa.* 48:6, *Isa.* 13:8, *Jer.* 6:24). This thought is present here, too, but uppermost in Paul's mind is probably the suddenness with which birth pangs come upon an expectant mother more or less without warning. The threatened destruction will break upon men and women in just that way.

And there will be no escape. Just as birth pains unavoidably come upon a mother-to-be, so there will be no escape from the Lord when he comes. Though people hide in caves in the mountains and call on rocks to cover them (*Rev.* 6:16), they will not evade his presence. Their judgement is inevitable.

The thought of this awesome day should arouse us as it evidently did the Thessalonian believers. It should make us deeply concerned for our unsuspecting relatives and neighbours. It should also stir us to be ready ourselves.

But just how should we prepare for that day? If it is not by identifying events that serve as signposts, or knowing precise dates, how can we get ready for it? The apostle will take up this very subject in the verses that follow.

21

Not Taken By Surprise

⁴But you, brothers, are not in darkness so that this day should surprise you like a thief. ⁵You are all sons of the light and sons of the day. We do not belong to the night or to the darkness. ⁶So then, let us not be like others, who are asleep, but let us be alert and self-controlled. ⁷For those who sleep, sleep at night, and those who get drunk, get drunk at night. ⁸But since we belong to the day, let us be self-controlled, putting on faith and love as a breastplate, and the hope of salvation as a helmet (1 Thess. 5:4–8).

The idea that the day of the Lord comes as a thief in the night naturally arouses dread. The suddenness and unexpectedness of the event are calculated to make the stoutest heart quake. Add to that the awful destruction that will overwhelm unsuspecting people, and you have a recipe for deep anxiety.

Paul, however, does not want his readers to be disturbed at the prospect of the Lord's return. The fact that they cannot know the exact day or hour when it will take place does not mean they should doubt their own safety or salvation when it does come. The verses in this section are aimed at assuring them of this.

NOT SURPRISED

First of all Paul tells the Thessalonian Christians that what he has been saying about the destructive, thief-like coming of the Lord does not apply to them. They belong to a different category of people from those who will be overwhelmed by judgement. Since they are 'brothers' (v.4), not those living in complacent 'peace and safety' (v.3), the day of the Lord will break upon them differently.

For one thing, it will not surprise them like a thief (v.4). True, they do not know the precise timing of the Lord's appearance, and so it will indeed come upon them with an element of surprise. But it will not be the surprise of total unexpectedness, the surprise of a thief invading without warning upon unsuspecting victims. Christians know the Lord is coming, and though he appears suddenly at a time when they are not anticipating him, his coming will not be a total surprise to them.

This is because they are not in darkness as other people are (v.4). Typically Paul uses the term 'darkness' to refer to spiritual ignorance and insensitivity. People who are in darkness do not know God and do not obey the gospel (*2 Thess.* 1:8). They live according to their lusts rather than God's light (*Eph.* 4:19) and are without God and without hope (*Eph.* 2:12). The day of the Lord will come upon them with the suddenness and unexpectedness of a thief because they have no idea at all about Jesus and God's purposes in him.

But this is not true of believers. By the grace of God, they are no longer living in darkness.

SONS OF LIGHT

On the contrary, Paul's readers are sons of the light and sons of the day, and do not belong to the darkness or the night (v.5). A great change has happened to Christians. They have moved from a realm of darkness to a realm of light.

Just as to be in darkness is to be spiritually ignorant and insensitive, so to be in the light is to be in a condition of knowledge, righteousness, acceptance and life. At conversion, God shines the light of his glory into the hearts of men and women (*2 Cor.* 4:6). They are immediately translated from a state of ignorance into a condition of knowing, from alienation to intimacy, and from hopelessness to eternal life.

More than that, they actually become 'sons' of the light and of the day (v.5). In ancient times, people were called 'sons' of something or someone when they shared its characteristics. Christians are sons of the light not only because they are in the light, but also because they have actually come to be like the light. Furthermore, the light has become their proper destiny. In Christ they are heirs of the kingdom of light (*Col.* 1:12). They have nothing more to do with the darkness.

In much the same way, they are sons of the day and do not belong to the night (v.5). The day in view is almost certainly the day of the Lord about which Paul has been speaking (v.2). Christians belong to that day in a special sense. It will be for them a day of resurrection and triumph. As the Lord descends from heaven Christians will meet with him in the air, and they will remain with him always (*1 Thess* 4:16–17). That day will fulfil all their hopes and complete Jesus' saving work (*John* 6:39).

The night which they have escaped, on the other hand, is the night of sin and judgement. All of us once belonged to the realm of darkness and faced the dreadful prospect of being swamped by the Lord's wrath (*Eph.* 2:3). But for Christians, that is no longer true. Even now, in Christ, we have entered into the new age of light and day (*Eph.* 5:8). We still look for the full and final revelation of that state, but it is nevertheless ours even now.

WATCHFUL AND SELF-CONTROLLED

That being so, we are to live as children of the light and of the day as we wait for the Lord to appear (v.6). Paul's point is that there is behaviour that belongs to the night and behaviour that belongs to the day. Those who belong to the night sleep and get drunk. Blissfully unaware of what is happening or about to happen, they indulge their sensual appetites. This is exactly how the unbelieving world lived in Paul's day, and it still does in our own (*Eph.* 2:3).

But Christians are not to be like others. As unpopular as it may be to stand apart from the crowd, we need to do so. We cannot live in the same way others do. Ours is not to be a lifestyle of slumber and drunkenness, but by contrast, we are to be self-controlled and alert.

The prospect of the Lord's coming should make us mentally alert and watchful. We are not to search frenetically for signs of his appearing, but we are always to live knowing that he will come soon. We are to be like soldiers watching vigilantly at our posts, fearful that we should be overtaken by the surprise visit of our commanding officer.

We are also to be self-controlled rather than drunk. This does not simply mean that we are to avoid getting intoxicated. It does mean that, of course, but more generally, Paul is saying that we need to be in control of all our faculties. We are to have them at our command and not allow ourselves to be mastered or dominated by excesses of any kind. We are to live temperate and balanced lives, not enslaved by our passions but rulers over them.

FAITH, LOVE AND HOPE

For Paul, the image of a soldier standing on watchful alert pictures perhaps better than anything the attitude Christians ought to have as they wait for the Lord. In keeping with that, he argues that far from allowing ourselves to sleep or become drunk, we are to be self-controlled, putting on faith and love as a breastplate, and the hope of salvation as a helmet (v.8).

Faith, love and hope are the spiritual armour that we are to wear as we wait for the Lord. Though we put these on at conversion, we need to go on clothing ourselves with them throughout our Christian lives. The best way to prepare ourselves for the Lord's coming is not by trying to fathom dates and times, but by ensuring that we are spiritually alert and well protected.

Faith and love are to serve as a breastplate for us, steadying and strengthening the heart, while the hope of our salvation is to act as a helmet, protecting the mind against doubt and despair. Well supplied with these, we will be able to stand and not be found wanting when Jesus returns.

22

No Need For Fear

*⁹For God did not appoint us to suffer wrath but to receive
salvation through our Lord Jesus Christ. ¹⁰He died for us so
that, whether we are awake or asleep, we may live together with
him. ¹¹Therefore encourage one another and build each other
up, just as in fact you are doing* (1 Thess. 5: 9–11).

M any Christians become more than a little apprehensive when
they think about the return of the Lord Jesus. They hope that
all will be well with them when he comes, but they are nevertheless
troubled by niggling fears about their safety in that day.

Sometimes those fears are the result of faulty or inadequate
teaching. Sometimes they are the product of natural timidity or a
languid spiritual life. Whatever the cause, Christians should not be
plagued by a lack of assurance when they think of the Lord's return.
They are to wait for his coming with eager confidence, wearing 'the
hope of salvation as a helmet' (v.8).

Paul wants believers in Thessalonica to enjoy this steady assurance
of approaching salvation as they wait for the Lord to appear. He
knows that some at least among them are timid (5:14), and he offers
strong grounds for confidence that the day of the Lord will be for
them a day of triumph rather than of terror.

APPOINTED TO SALVATION, NOT WRATH

Ultimately, our hope of being saved in the day of the Lord rests in
God's purpose or appointment. We have already noted that Paul
refers to his Thessalonian converts as those who have been loved,

chosen and called by God (*1 Thess.* 1:4; 2:12). He traces their believing response to the gospel not to their intellect or moral sensitivity, but to God's plan for them. They have been chosen by him in eternity (*Eph.* 1:4) and called by him in time (*Rom.* 8:28–30). He wants them to know that from beginning to end their salvation is anchored deeply in God's initiative and plan.

In harmony with that, he now says that the God who has loved, chosen and called them has destined them not to suffer wrath but to obtain salvation (v.9). He has chosen us to be holy and blameless before him and predestined us to be his adopted sons (*Eph.* 1:4–5).

Every Christian can rejoice in this certainty. If we can say with any confidence at all that we belong to the Lord – that through his gracious call we have heard and believed the gospel and become his loved children – then we can be sure that we are guaranteed of salvation and not wrath when the Lord returns.

CONTRASTING DESTINIES

We do well to consider for a moment the two destinies – wrath and salvation – that face mankind in the future.

(i) For all who are not God's people, the day of the Lord will be a day of fierce wrath. While we must not think of God's wrath in terms of the unbridled, uncontrolled passion of human anger, we must not shrink from recognising anger as a characteristic of the God of the Bible. His anger is the response to sin of his infinitely holy love. He cannot look upon sin and be anything but passionately opposed to it (*Hab.*1:13, *1 John* 1:5).

His wrath toward unrepentant sinners is his just response to their sinfulness. The day of the Lord will mark the end of his patience toward them. On that day the full measure of his anger will be poured out on all who have despised his merciful provision of pardon in Christ.

Most of us have at some time trembled before the merited wrath of a parent or a teacher. The passion of their anger silenced all resistance on our part, and the justness of their cause left us defenceless before their punishment. The mere recollection of such experiences is enough to make us shudder. Yet as awful as they may have been, they cannot compare with the experience of meeting the

Lord in the fury of his wrath on the day of his coming. Who can but dread such an encounter!

(ii) But for those who believe, the coming day of the Lord will be a day to receive the salvation God has appointed for them. Here Paul is thinking of salvation in its final and fullest sense, sometimes referred to by scholars as eschatological salvation. While it is true that as believers we experience salvation now through faith in the gospel, it is also true that our salvation is something still to come. It is that salvation that Paul says we will receive when Jesus returns.

Any view of salvation that is limited to present enjoyment of pardon falls short of the fuller biblical picture. God's salvation finds fulfilment in the restored universe, in the perfected kingdom to come.

SALVATION THROUGH CHRIST

It would be entirely wrong, however, to suppose that when Paul speaks of his readers receiving (or, more literally, 'attaining') salvation at the appearing of the Lord, he has in mind any thought of them actually meriting or earning that salvation. Their destiny is to receive salvation through our Lord Jesus Christ (v.9). Their entitlement to that salvation depends upon God's purpose accomplished through the work of his Son Jesus.

We enjoy salvation only because he died for us (v.10). There was no other way in which we could be made fit for God's kingdom and made ready to be his sons. The wrath we so richly deserve by nature (*Eph.* 2:3), and which we have seen will be experienced by unbelievers in the day of the Lord, had to be averted through the payment for our sins. Our sinful nature also had to be renewed and our enslavement to the powers of passion and darkness broken. All this could be, and was, accomplished only through the death of the Lord Jesus Christ. Familiar though the idea of Jesus' death might be, it must always remain the basis of our hope. Well might Paul write, 'May I never boast except in the cross of our Lord Jesus Christ' (*Gal.* 6:14). Our hope of salvation rests upon it alone.

Through his cross the Lord Jesus secured more than endless existence for his people. He obtained the full salvation that God planned for them from before time began (*Titus* 1:2). He died for us, Paul writes, so that, whether we are alive or dead when he comes, we may live together with him (v.10). Here the apostle describes that salvation as living together with Christ. The summit of spiritual blessing in the age to come lies in the unbroken presence and fellowship of the Lord Jesus. Made like him (*Rom.* 8:29), we shall share his glory as heirs together of the new heaven and new earth (*Rom.* 8:17). This is the scope of the salvation that awaits all who believe the gospel of God concerning his Son.

WORDS FULL OF COMFORT

Not surprisingly, Paul ends this discussion of the day of the Lord by instructing the Thessalonians to encourage one another and build each other up (v.11). They are to encourage one another as they struggle with doubts and fears connected with the coming day of the Lord. From what Paul has written, they know that they need not dread being found unprepared. The day of the Lord will not surprise them as it will others.

Furthermore, they are to build one another up through what they have learned. Spiritual growth is always the best antidote to anxiety. They now have ample insight into the things to come to ward off anxiety concerning the return of Christ. They need now to use the knowledge they have, to talk about it with one another and absorb its implications for their lives. They must not rely on teachers and apostles to do this for them; they are perfectly capable of doing it among themselves, as they have already shown. In the church, the ministry of encouragement can never be left to a select few. All believers are able to do it, and all need to do it.

This, then, is how we are to wait for the coming of the Lord. We are not to be distracted into sign-seeking or time-keeping. Rather, we are to keep alert and self-controlled, always alive with the confident hope that the coming day will bring to us the salvation of being for ever with the Lord.

23

Getting On with One Another

¹²Now we ask you, brothers, to respect those who work hard among you, who are over you in the Lord and who admonish you. ¹³Hold them in the highest regard in love because of their work. Live in peace with each other. ¹⁴And we urge you, brothers, warn those who are idle, encourage the timid, help the weak, be patient with everyone. ¹⁵Make sure that nobody pays back wrong for wrong, but always try to be kind to each other and to everyone else (1 Thess. 5:12–15).

P aul has not finished what he has to say to the church in Thessalonica. Pressing matters of ethical and moral concern have been addressed; so, too, have important issues relating to the second coming of the Lord. But up until this point scarcely a word has been said about everyday life within the congregation. It is to this the apostle turns in the closing section of his letter.

What he has to say is contained in a series of short compressed appeals and commands. To what degree they reflect existing problems in the church is uncertain. Paul may have considered them essential encouragement for all congregations whatever their circumstances (cf. *Rom.* 12:9–21). At the same time, traces of problems throughout the earlier part of this letter suggest that the apostle might have been putting his pastoral finger on trouble spots in the life of the congregation.

WITH LEADERS

He begins with a note of warm appeal. 'Now we ask you, brothers' (v.12), he says, not simply wanting to signal a change of topic, but to make a genuine plea for action. He wants to discuss a number of practical matters, and he asks for the full attention and hearty response of his readers to them.

The first concerns the way they relate to their leaders (vv.12–13). Although the apostle does not give any title or official rank to those he has in mind, clearly they are the spiritual leaders of the young church. They are people who are in a position of being over them in the Lord, an expression that points to a role of authoritative rule and responsible care. They are, furthermore, those who admonish them, who correct them when they are erring by calling to mind the right way of the Lord. And because this kind of care is as arduous as any form of manual labour, they are also spoken of as those who work hard (toil to the point of weariness) among them.

The brothers in the congregation are to show these people respect, or, as the word is often translated, they are to 'know' them. They are to observe closely the quality of their personal lives and work, and to regard them with esteem and affection on account of these. More than that, they are to hold them in the highest regard in love (v.13). Paul struggles to express adequately the strength of esteem they are to have for their leaders. Ideas like 'beyond', 'exceedingly', and 'abundantly' are all crammed into the language he uses. He is not advocating a servile deference towards leaders, but an attitude of deep affection and appreciation.

This is because of their work (v.13). Church leaders watch over the spiritual welfare of those entrusted to them as those who must one day give account to their Master (*Heb.*13:17). Theirs is a difficult and often intensely painful task. Appreciative and affectionate relationships make it so much easier and more pleasant. They also make it more profitable.

Perhaps it is on that account that the apostle adds the further charge that the members of the church live in peace with each other. Peace enables leaders to do their work well. Where they must toil in the face of quarrels and strife, resentment and rebellion, their work becomes almost unbearable. The importance of Christians striving to keep the unity of the Spirit in the bond of peace cannot be over-emphasised (*Eph.* 4:3).

WITH THE NEEDY

Leaving the subject of relationships with their leaders, Paul now instructs the congregation in the way it is to respond to three classes of people within it: the idle, the timid, and the weak (v.14). These might well be called the problem children of the congregation, distinct groups of people with special characteristics and needs, who place special demands upon the church.

The idle are probably the loafers referred to earlier, members who have 'broken rank' (as the term means) with the rest of the congregation by refusing to work (4:11; *2 Thess.* 3:11). The timid are those who lack courage in the face of persecution or other unknowns, such as events at the second coming of Christ. The weak are almost certainly those inclined to crumble when faced with either moral temptations (4:3–8) or spiritual scruples (*1 Cor.* 8:9–13).

The brothers are to respond to each in ways appropriate to their case. They are to warn the idle, admonishing and instructing them to correct their faulty behaviour. They are to encourage the timid, coming alongside them offering the strength of well-chosen words of comfort in the midst of their fears (4:18; 5:11). And they are to help the weak, cleaving to them closely so as to be on hand in times of temptation and trial.

This is to be done showing patience to everyone (v.14). Quick fixes seldom remedy deep faults. As trying as the needy may be in a congregation, they are not to be brushed off or deserted. On the contrary, they are to be borne with great patience.

This responsibility, it should be noted, is shared by the entire congregation and is not to be left to the 'professionals'. Recognised leaders do indeed have a special role in warning, encouraging and helping (v.12). But the task is not theirs alone. It might even be more correct to say that their work is not so much to do these things as to see they are done (by others). The ascended Lord gave leaders to the church not to rob members of their ministries, but to fit them for ministry (*Eph.* 4:12).

WITH THOSE WHO WRONG US

Paul adds a further important admonition, the call to non-retaliation (v.15). Given the severe persecution the Thessalonians were suffering and the inevitable offences that form part of living closely with others in community, Paul's readers probably had special need of this reminder. Retaliation is an instinct of our sinful nature, especially when we are under stress. Yet it is an instinct condemned by the gospel. Vengeance belongs to the Lord, not to the party who has been wronged (*Rom.* 12:17–19).

Rather than retaliate when wronged, we must always try to be kind to each other and everyone else (v.15). Passive submission to wrongdoing is not what is required of us. We must do all that we can, expending every ounce of our energy, to return good for evil – and not only to those within the Christian congregation, but to everyone. A forbearing spirit is to be displayed toward even the most unlovely and hostile of our enemies. Only the grace of Christ can enable us to do this (*Phil.* 4:13).

Relationships do count for Christians. We must live with our leaders, with our fellow believers, and with the non-Christian world in ways that reflect the power of the gospel. Tragically, those of us most concerned with correct doctrine often fail abysmally in the way we relate to other people. Paul's words offer rebuke and correction on that point.

24

Christian Spiritual Life

¹⁶Be joyful always; ¹⁷pray continually; ¹⁸give thanks in all circumstances, for this is God's will for you in Christ Jesus.
¹⁹Do not put out the Spirit's fire; ²⁰do not treat prophecies with contempt. ²¹Test everything. Hold on to the good. ²²Avoid every kind of evil (1 Thess. 5:16–22).

'Last but not least' is a saying so well-worn that it has practically lost its meaning. We use it unthinkingly. These final exhortations of Paul's first letter to the Thessalonians, however, are one instance in which it is supremely applicable.

For most of the letter up to this point, Paul's attention has been occupied with pressing personal, moral and social needs in the congregation. Only as these have been dealt with and laid aside does he address what might be called the more directly spiritual aspects of the life of the congregation. Yet far from unimportant, they are the wellspring of the church's life. Without a thriving inner life, the church will never fulfil its moral and social obligations in the world. Holy living can flow only from a healthy heart.

JOY, PRAYER AND THANKFULNESS

Three short commands allow us to pinpoint activities that should characterise the spiritual life of every Christian. Paul wants his readers to be joyful always, to pray continually, and to give thanks in all circumstances (vv. 16–18). Joy, prayer and thanksgiving should mark the life of the Christian community, both in its individual and in its corporate expression.

Joy is an especially notable feature of New Testament Christianity. Typically, the good news of the gospel brought joy to those who received it. This was far more than the momentary happiness that we often associate with joy. It was a lasting, deep-seated sense of well-being and pleasure produced by the Holy Spirit now living within them (*Luke* 10:21, *Gal.* 5:22). The Thessalonian Christians themselves had experienced this even as they suffered persecution for their newly found faith (1:6). Indeed, it was the presence of radiant joy in suffering that attracted many in the pagan world to the early Christians.

Paul wants his readers in Thessalonica to demonstrate that joy always. He actually commands them to be joyful, even at all times and in all circumstances. This reinforces the idea that spiritual joy is more than human happiness. Happiness cannot be turned off and on at will. Christian joy, however, is a conscious attitude of rejoicing in the Lord and in what he has done. It does not depend ultimately upon our feelings or circumstances. We may not always feel buoyant and cheerful, yet we can deliberately call to mind the Lord and rejoice in him at all times (*Phil.* 4:4).

This quality of constancy is also to mark prayer life. The apostle instructs his converts to pray continually (v.17). He assumes that they know about prayer and that they are already a praying people. Non-praying Christians, after all, are an anomaly. Prayer, like joy, is a spontaneous feature of true faith. Where it is missing, faith is also absent, or at best, weak.

It is continual prayer that he is seeking. He wants his readers to be in a constant frame of dependence upon God, even when they are not engaged in specific acts of prayer. They are not to limit prayer to particular times in the day or to occasions when they meet together as a congregation. They are to live in an atmosphere of intimacy with God. Their hearts are to be lifted up to him even when their hands and minds are busy with other tasks. Like Enoch and Noah, they are to walk with God (*Gen.* 5:24; 6:9).

Their lives should be marked by gratitude, too. They are to give thanks in all circumstances (v.18). Believing that their lives are in the hands of a wise and holy Father and that all things, seemingly good and bad, come from him, they are to be thankful. This is true Christianity!

Again, foremost in this command is the element of constancy. The Thessalonian Christians probably thought they had plenty of reasons to be miserable and self-pitying. Yet Paul insists that they should be thankful in all circumstances. They are to see the good hand of God in all that happens to them and believe that he is working all things together for their good (*Rom.* 8:28).

Ingratitude is always a sign of unbelief. Faith recognises that God is at work for our good and his glory in even the most seemingly adverse situations. It enables us to say thank you even through tears.

These three things, then – joy, prayer and thankfulness – are to be part of our everyday, all-day life. They are God's will for us in Christ Jesus (v.18). This is the way those who are in Christ Jesus are to live. Is it the way we are living?

HONOURING THE SPIRIT

From what might be termed general, common features of Christian spirituality, Paul turns next to things that belong to the corporate life of the church. He has in mind especially the ministry of the Holy Spirit in the congregation. The gift of the Spirit was a striking and treasured feature of the life of the early church, and the apostle wants the congregation in Thessalonica to honour his presence.

He warns them not to put out the Spirit's fire (v.19). The Holy Spirit had come with the sign of fire at Pentecost (*Acts* 2:3) and continued to fuel the church's life with warmth and light. Anything that repressed his work might fittingly be described as quenching or putting out his fire.

Paul does not explain in detail how that might be done. Perhaps he is warning against envy and covetousness in respect to the special gifts of the Spirit (*1 Cor.* 12, 14). Or he may be thinking more broadly of the way we can dishonour the Spirit by ignoring his presence or resisting his leading. Whatever he has in mind, he implies that Christians can hinder the Spirit's influence by their attitudes and actions. And he warns sternly against that.

Paul's readers are to be especially careful about the way they respond to prophecy in the congregation. One of the ways in which the Holy Spirit nourished the life of the early church was through the gift of prophecy. This was a speaking gift that helped the congregation learn and understand God's word. Paul ranks it very highly because it contributed so directly to the building up of the church (*1 Cor.* 14:1–5).

Here he tells the Thessalonian believers that they are not to treat prophecies with contempt (v.20). They were perhaps in danger of doing so. It is not difficult to imagine how such a fault might have arisen. The excitement so evident in the congregation surrounding the Lord's return could easily have spawned claims to prophetic messages about the event. While such 'prophecies' would have thrilled some, they would likely have offended others, damaging the very status of the gift itself in the life of the church.

Sadly, the abuse of spiritual gifts often exposes them to contempt. Questionable claims to miracles and prophecies discredit genuine expressions of God's power.

SPIRITUAL DISCERNMENT

Whether or not there was an actual problem with prophecy in the church in Thessalonica, Paul makes it clear that the gift itself is to be prized. If it was subject to abuse, people were not to respond by despising it but by testing all claimed revelations.

They were to test everything (v.21), much in the same way that they might examine a metal or gemstone to test its purity. That which they found to be good, they were to hold on to (v.21), but everything that was evil, they were to avoid or stand aloof from (v.22). The gifts of the Spirit were to be valued but exercised with discernment. Sadly, not everything claimed to be from the Spirit was indeed of the Spirit. The counterfeit co-existed with the true.

Our day has seen a welcome resurgence of interest in the ministry of the Holy Spirit in the church. There can be no expectation of blessing where he is not honoured and where his presence is not actively sought. But with revived interest in the Spirit there has also arisen the urgent need for discernment. Bizarre claims are in danger of fostering contempt for the Spirit and his gifts today just as they did in the first century. We are not to respond to these with uncritical gullibility, but nor are we to reject every claim that the Spirit is at work. Paul would have us test all things, holding to the good but rejecting the evil.

The church through the ages has been strong only when it has recognised that its life lies in God himself. When it has done this, its emphasis has not been upon its activities, its buildings, or its organisation. Rather, worship and prayer for mighty manifestations of the Holy Spirit have been the focus of its energies. This remains the path to spiritual strength today.

25

Sanctification and Security

²³May God himself, the God of peace, sanctify you through and through. May your whole spirit, soul and body be kept blameless at the coming of our Lord Jesus Christ. ²⁴The one who calls you is faithful and he will do it (1 Thess. 5:23–24).

From the beginning of the fourth chapter to this point in his letter, Paul has been absorbed with counselling and encouraging the Christians in Thessalonica. He has done so to help them become more mature and settled in the faith. As God's chosen people (1:4), they have been called to live holy lives in this world (4:3) and to share in his kingdom and glory (2:12) when Jesus returns. Paul sees his role to be one of helping them walk worthy of such a calling.

Nothing could be more natural in the light of this than that the apostle should end his letter with a fervent prayer wish for their sanctification and security. He has explained how they are to live and how they are to prepare themselves for the coming of the Lord. Now he looks to the one who alone can enable them to act as they ought.

TOTAL SANCTIFICATION

He prays firstly for their sanctification. The idea of sanctification has been behind much of what Paul has written in the last two chapters. We have already noted that he began a series of ethical instructions by saying that it was God's will that they should be sanctified (4:3). This follows from being chosen to be God's people (1:4). Because he is holy, they, too, must be holy (*Lev.* 11:45, *1 Pet.* 1:16).

Paul prays that the process of sanctification would be brought to completion. He wants them to be sanctified 'through and through' (v.23).

He is well aware that in Christ they are already completely set apart to God and accepted as holy (*1 Cor.* 1:2). But it is not this aspect of sanctification he is thinking about. He is referring to the process of transformation that takes place in the life of a Christian as a result of being united to Christ.

This had begun in his readers, but Paul longs for it to progress further. Indeed, he wants it to be accomplished thoroughly in a way that affects the whole of their being. Paul never taught that it was possible that people could live perfect, sinless lives in this world. But he was an idealist in this respect. He knew that God's standard was perfect sanctification and that one day every Christian would be completely sanctified.

His prayer reflects that understanding. He cannot be content with people taking just the first steps toward a holy life. He wants to see his converts renewed through and through. Complete sanctification should be the goal of every true believer.

THE SANCTIFYING GOD

Paul does not suppose, however, that this work of transformation is something his readers can accomplish themselves. He prays that God himself, the God of peace (v.23), would bring it about.

In saying this, he acknowledges that sanctification is God's work. True, there is a human dimension to it, reflected in the commands and instructions Paul has already given (4:1). God addresses us as those who are responsible to live as he commands. We are expected to turn from old sinful patterns of life to the new way of life we learn in Christ (*Eph.* 4:20–24). The Bible nowhere teaches that sanctification takes place without human involvement and effort.

But neither does it teach that it is possible to be sanctified in the least degree by human will or effort alone. It is only through God the Holy Spirit working in us that we can make any progress at all toward holiness. He is the one behind every good wish and desire that we experience, and he supplies the inner resolve to do what we know to be his will (*Phil.* 2:13, *2 Thess.* 1:11–12; 2:13). In effect, it is God who is the great sanctifier of his people.

In this connection, Paul refers to God as the God of peace, a designation he often uses in his letters (*Rom.* 15:33; 16:20, *2 Cor.* 13:11).

It points to the perfect wholeness and rest that God knows in himself, and alludes to the same wholeness that he brings to sinners through his Son Jesus Christ. The God of peace is the God of salvation, the one who establishes peace in its fullest sense by saving and sanctifying sinners.

God's peace is always bound up with holiness. We can never know his peace in any sense at all as long as we are alienated from him through sin. Then as believers, we enjoy the conscious experience of that peace only as we live in his ways.

BLAMELESS IN HIS PRESENCE

But the apostle's focus in his letter has not been on sanctification or holiness alone. He has also said much about the second coming of the Lord Jesus. In fact, the two themes have been closely intertwined (3:13). It is at the second coming that we enter fully into the experience of being God's holy people. This creates the atmosphere of hope (1:3) so characteristic of the Christian faith.

In keeping with that, Paul also prays that his readers will be kept blameless at the coming of the Lord Jesus Christ (v.23). Since the Lord comes to judge the world and execute his Father's wrath upon sinners, nothing is more critical than that we should be prepared for his arrival. We are to pass through the judgement and enter into the glory that lies beyond (*Luke* 21:36). And if that is to be so, we must be kept blameless in our whole spirit, soul and body (v.23).

These latter words have generated a wealth of discussion. Many see in them a description of the component parts of man – spirit, soul and body. Others protest that the Bible consistently speaks of people having a body along with a soul or spirit, the terms 'spirit' and 'soul' referring essentially to the same entity. We cannot enter into the technicalities of this debate. We can be sure, however, that Paul did not intend to provide here a formal analysis of our human makeup.

What he is saying is that when the Lord comes, we need to be found blameless in every aspect of our lives. For at that time the Lord Jesus will not only scrutinise people outwardly (the deeds of their bodies), but also judge their innermost secrets (*Rom.* 2:1, *1 Cor.* 4:5). We will need to be found blameless in our outward actions, in our self-conscious thoughts and desires, and in our relationship with God himself.

This is not meant to suggest that in the end our salvation will hinge on our personal character and works. We know that no one will be saved from wrath and eternal death through their own works. Our ultimate destiny is decided on the basis of what the Lord Jesus himself has done for us and upon our union with him through faith (*Rom.* 3:20–26).

Nevertheless, believers, too, must stand before the judgement seat of Christ and be assessed for what they have done while living in the body (*2 Cor.* 5:10). We shall have to give account for all that we have thought, said and done. This is the apostle's concern. He wants his cherished converts in Thessalonica to be able to stand before the Lord with confidence and joy rather than in dread and shame.

THE FAITHFUL GOD

But how can we, so sinful and liable to stumble, hope to appear blameless before the Lord? Thankfully, it does not depend upon us. The apostle speaks of his Thessalonian readers 'being kept blameless' at the coming of the Lord (v.23). He then states more fully that the one who calls is faithful and he will do it (v.24). In the end, our security rests in the Lord himself. He is the one who is able to keep us from falling and present us before his glorious presence without fault and with great joy (*Jude* 24).

As we have seen more than once, our salvation is rooted in the election and calling of God. He chooses, and he calls in accord with that choice. The point Paul now makes is that the one who calls is also faithful – faithful to his purposes, and his covenant promises. What he had determined he will surely accomplish (*Isa.* 46:10). What he has promised, he will surely perform. Our certainty of being able to stand before the Lord rests finally not in ourselves, but in God himself. He will do it!

We are left, as we end our study of this prayer, with a very clear appreciation of what mattered most to Paul. It was not, as is so often the case with us, the temporal needs of his converts connected with their present existence. It was rather their spiritual readiness to meet and be with the Lord. This ought to be our priority, too.

26

Final Words

*²⁵Brothers, pray for us. ²⁶Greet all the brothers with a holy kiss.
²⁷I charge you before the Lord to have this letter read to all
the brothers. ²⁸The grace of our Lord Jesus Christ be with you*
(1 Thess. 5:25–28).

In our haste to finish reading Paul's letters we often skim the closing
verse or two, especially if they contain a series of brief, personalised
instructions about housekeeping matters, as is the case in this letter.

We can never do so, however, without running the risk of over-
looking something valuable. In Christ everything takes on new
meaning, even the most commonplace of daily activities. In touching
on some of these practical matters as he finishes his letters, Paul often
provides us with key insights into how the gospel is to affect daily
living.

In this case he closes with a request, two instructions, and a
benediction, all of which are laden with helpful instruction.

A PLEA FOR PRAYER

His request is a plea for prayer for himself and his associates, Silas
and Timothy. 'Brothers,' he writes, deliberately addressing the
Thessalonians in this way to remind them again of their bonds in
Christ, 'pray for us' (v.25). The three missionaries have been praying
ceaselessly for the church in Thessalonica (1:2, 3; 3:10). Now Paul
asks that it reciprocate and pray for them.

That he should make such a request shows his remarkable
humility. Apostle though he was, and veteran of many gospel battles,
Paul did not regard it beneath his dignity to ask the help of raw

converts to the faith. They were brothers and sisters in Christ after all, part of the same family of God. As such, they all belonged to each other as helpers in the faith and the ministry of the gospel (*Rom.* 12:5). Greater maturity and experience should never become a bar to being ministered to by those newer in the faith. Elitism has no place in the church of the Lord Jesus.

That he should ask them to pray also shows how aware Paul was of his dependence on the grace of God in his ministry. Daily he and his helpers were faced with superhuman demands. The only way they could meet these challenges was through the grace of God. And the only means of laying hold of that grace was through believing prayer. Prayer is not peripheral to gospel ministry, an add-on to the larger tasks of preaching and counselling and evangelism. It forms the very heart of the work itself as God's appointed means of obtaining his necessary power.

Paul was always ready to enlist the help of others in prayer because he knew the value of intercession (*Phil.* 1:19, *2 Cor.* 1:11). God does not hear only the prayers we offer for ourselves. He also hears his family at prayer for one another. Indeed, the Lord Jesus encouraged his disciples to pray in a way that highlighted their solidarity when he taught them to pray, '*Our* Father in heaven . . . give *us* . . . forgive *us* . . . lead *us* . . . deliver *us*' (*Matt.* 6: 9–13). If we are wise, we will be quick to enlist the help of others through prayer. We will also undertake the costly ministry of intercession ourselves.

GUIDELINES FOR GREETINGS

From a request, Paul turns to a command. He wants the Christians in Thessalonica to be sure to 'greet all the brothers with a holy kiss' (v.26).

The practice of greeting one another was as common in ancient societies as it is in our own. The Christian gospel did not demand that customs like this be done away with, but it gave them new meaning. When Christians encountered one another, they were not merely fellow citizens meeting. They were fellow members in God's family who belonged to each other in Christ. How fitting, then, that they should not only greet one another, but greet in a way that reflected their relationship.

Here Paul says they are to greet one another with a holy kiss. Kissing was a common form of greeting at that time, and Christians were to continue to use it as part of their life together. However, their kiss of greeting was to be holy, that is, one that reflected the gospel. It was to be the affectionate kiss of family members who related to one another with utter moral purity. Later abuses of this practice required that it first be restricted and then eventually curtailed altogether.

Paul wants this form of greeting to be extended not just to some of the brothers, but to all of them. Given the size of the congregation, he may have meant that everyone was to be sure to greet everyone else whenever they met together. It may be, however, that he wanted them to avoid selectivity in their greeting. They were not to greet just their close friends in the church and ignore those who were less appealing. Since all belonged to the family of God, all, no matter who they were, should be greeted with the same inward warmth and outward affection. He is warning against the partiality that so quickly hardens into factions and cliques within the church. The practice of greeting everyone in the same way acts as a powerful counter to this damaging tendency.

Too little attention is given to the practice of Christian greeting today. The perfunctory way in which we so often greet one another falls far short of what Paul has in mind. It should be a matter of conscience to us to greet fellow Christians in a way that reflects our relation to them and our affection for them. The Christian church, after all, is not to be a collection of floating individuals, but a community of love bound together in its common faith by cords of sincere affection. And this is to find expression in warm greetings.

READING THE LETTER

Paul has one more instruction to add, and this concerns the reading of the letter itself (v.27). This is no light request but has the strength of a demand made on oath. The Lord himself bears witness to what he is asking them to do.

Paul evidently wants to guard against his letter becoming the restricted property of a select few within the church. Perhaps it was to be conveyed to the leaders of the church (5:12), but it was most certainly not meant just for them, and must not become closeted with them. The apostle has all the members of the church on his heart (1:1, 2). He longs to be with them to establish them in the faith (3:10), but in his circumstances he cannot (2:18). This letter must make up for his personal presence. It was intended to be a means of instruction and blessing to all, and consequently, it was to be read to all.

While not specifying that this take place at one of the regular assemblies of the church on the Lord's Day, we may assume that Paul had something like this in view. Records of early church worship show that apostolic letters quickly gained a place alongside the Old Testament Scriptures in public reading in Christian meetings. This in turn contributed to their acceptance as Scripture and their eventual inclusion in the canon of our Bible. The practice of reading and explaining these letters in Christian gatherings continues today. They are the divinely given source of instruction and must continue to be studied until the Lord returns.

PAUL'S FAREWELL

Paul is ready to sign off his letter. He has a convention that he can follow, but as with his initial greeting, he does not conform to it slavishly but Christianises it.

Letter writers of Paul's day usually ended their letters by saying 'farewell' or 'goodbye'. In essence, this was a wish for good health and fortune. The writer was expressing his hope that his reader would 'fare well'. Paul, however, is not interested in his readers simply faring well. As sincerely as he might wish their health and wealth, he has a much greater desire for them. He would rather that the grace of the Lord Jesus Christ be with them (v.28).

For Paul, the Christian life was a life of grace, saturated from beginning to end with the undeserved favour and blessing of God. It began in grace, was sustained by grace, and would be consummated through grace. It is this grace, residing so fully in the Lord Jesus Christ for his church (*John* 1:16), that the apostle wants the Thessalonians to enjoy in abundance. He wants them, in other words, to be filled with the life of Christ.

How vastly superior this is to a mere 'good-health' wish. It highlights again how different our lives should be as Christians. Even our common 'hello' and 'goodbye' should reflect that our lives are bound up with Christ. Is that true of us?

On this fitting note, Paul ends what has been an intensely pastoral letter. Addressed though it was to a first-century church in a distinct historical context, it nevertheless speaks with amazing directness to us today. It offers instruction in evangelism, ministry and worship and provides encouragement to us in our trials. But perhaps above all, it challenges us as God's chosen people to live in ways that please him (4:1) as we wait in confident hope for his Son to appear from heaven.

2 Thessalonians

I

A Second Letter

¹Paul, Silas and Timothy, To the church of the Thessalonians in God our Father and the Lord Jesus Christ: ²Grace and peace to you from God the Father and the Lord Jesus Christ (2 Thess. 1:1–2).

Some time after Paul dispatched the letter we have just finished studying, he found need to write again to the church in Thessalonica. We do not know how long the time gap was between the two letters, but it may have been a matter of only weeks or, at the longest, a few months.

Some suggest that the second was prompted by a letter from the leaders of the church. According to this view, a fresh crisis had arisen in the congregation, a crisis the local leaders did not feel capable of handling. Hearing that one of their members was travelling to Corinth, they outlined the problem in a letter and asked the apostle to provide help.

While we cannot know for sure that this was how the letter came to be written, we can say confidently that it was written in response to needs in the congregation. 2 Thessalonians, like its earlier companion letter, is intensely pastoral and practical in nature.

The contents of the letter itself show that at least three issues were troubling the church. The first was ongoing (and perhaps intensified) persecution (1:3–10). The second was a troublesome rumour supposedly originating from Paul himself alleging that the day of the Lord had already come (2:1–2). And the third was the continuing irritation caused by a section of the church that refused to work (3:6–15).

[119]

ONGOING SUFFERING

We have already noted that the church in Thessalonica had its birth in suffering. The missionaries themselves had been harassed and were eventually forced to leave the city (*Acts* 17:5–9), and the new converts had experienced opposition as they turned from idols to serve the true God (*1 Thess.* 1:6–9). Concern over this had caused deep anguish for Paul and his helpers during their enforced absence from the church (*1 Thess.* 3:3–5).

Conditions had not improved in the time between the two letters. If anything, they had worsened. The Thessalonian Christians were forced to live out their new faith in a climate of stiff persecution and trial (*2 Thess.* 1:3). They were evidently doing this with great patience and courage. However, unrelieved suffering often promotes despair, or at least perplexity. Young Christians can be confused when God allows them to suffer. It raises questions and doubts about his goodness and faithfulness, and even about their own relationship to him. Perhaps some of the believers in Thessalonica were struggling in this way.

Paul meets this particular need in the opening paragraphs of his letter. He assures his readers that their firmness under suffering is a cause of great joy to himself and his fellow workers, and that they boast freely of them among other churches (1:4). They need not be perplexed about God's purpose in what they are suffering, because the time will come when his justice will be made clear to everyone. They need to wait patiently for God himself to right wrongs and deliver them from trouble.

UNHELPFUL RUMOURS

A second reason for writing had to do with rumours about the day of the Lord, or the *parousia*. We have already seen how prominently this event featured in the minds of the Thessalonians. They had been taught about it and were eagerly looking for it, but were also somewhat apprehensive about it (*1 Thess.* 4:13–5:11).

Somehow a report had reached the Thessalonians that Paul was saying that the day of the Lord had already come (*2 Thess.* 2:2). This would naturally have alarmed the faint-hearted members of the congregation. They had been concerned enough about what would happen to those who had already died in the Lord, and they were anxious about their own readiness to meet the Lord Jesus when he returned. How would they respond to claims that he had already come?

Paul addresses this problem head on (2:3–12). He tells his readers that the day of the Lord cannot come until there has first been a great rebellion. That in turn will not take place until 'the man of lawlessness' has been revealed. But he cannot be revealed until that which is currently holding him back is taken away. In short, a series of events must happen before the day of the Lord can come.

This perspective on the Lord's coming causes some people to question whether Paul is in fact the author of both 1 and 2 Thessalonians. In 1 Thessalonians, the argument goes, the writer speaks of the day of the Lord as though it were imminent, something that might happen at any moment. But in this second letter, Paul insists that it is still some time off and will happen only at the climax of a series of other events. Could the same writer have viewed the one event in such conflicting ways?

The simple answer to this is, Yes, indeed he could. The two perspectives are not in conflict; both are true. Different needs required that Paul emphasise one in his first letter and the other in his second. We always need to be aware that in Paul's letters especially, statements addressing particular needs are often partial expressions of a larger truth.

PERSISTENT REBELLION

The third concern that emerges in this letter has to do with the people in the congregation described earlier as idlers (*1 Thess.* 5:14). We concluded that they were probably a group of people who, in their excitement over the return of the Lord Jesus, had stopped working and had become interfering, troublesome busybodies.

The apostle had spelt out their duty in his first letter. They were to aim to live quiet and productive lives (*1 Thess.* 4:11,12), taking care not to become dependent upon anybody. This should have been sufficient to settle this disorder.

Apparently, however, it was not. The sharp references to such people in this letter indicate that they had not heeded the earlier instructions. Perhaps the intensified persecution and talk about the arrival of the day of the Lord had only strengthened their conviction that there was no point in working to provide for the future.

Paul, however, disagrees. He has no time for loafing fanatics. The church is told how to deal with them and authorised to take measures that at least approach excommunication (3:6–14). Unruliness of this sort had to be stopped.

FAMILIAR GREETINGS

As best as we can reconstruct from the letter itself, that seems to have been the situation in Thessalonica that prompted Paul to write again.

The opening words of his second letter are almost identical to those of his first.

(i) The writers are the same three men, Paul, Silas and Timothy, and they are introduced in the same simple, unqualified way (v.1). The three were evidently still together when Paul dictated this letter, probably still in Corinth.

(ii) The church itself is addressed in almost identical terms. Here Paul substitutes God *our* Father for God *the* Father in his first letter to highlight that in this instance he is thinking of God as the Father of believers rather than of our Lord Jesus Christ. Through faith his readers have become sons of God along with all other believers. They were now part of the one household and family of God (*Eph.* 3:15, *1 Tim.* 3:15).

(iii) The blessing, apart from an added ending, is also the same (v.2). Grace and peace, as we saw in the first letter, are the sum of God's spiritual blessings for his people. Here Paul affirms that they come to them from God the Father and from his Son, a fact omitted (according to some manuscripts) in the earlier letter.

That the Father and Son are linked as the source of spiritual blessing to the church points once more to the high view the apostles had of the person of the Lord Jesus Christ. He, no less than the Father, is the source of the grace and peace that gives them life. To put him on a level of equality with God can be possible only if he is indeed one with God.

With these familiar words Paul re-establishes contact with his much-loved converts in Thessalonica. He is still vitally interested in their welfare. The process of discipling them will stop only when he sees them fully mature in Christ (*Col.* 1:28). Meanwhile he will stint no effort to relieve their fears, correct their errors and encourage their obedience.

2

Gratitude for Growth

³We ought always to thank God for you, brothers, and rightly so, because your faith is growing more and more, and the love every one of you has for each other is increasing. ⁴Therefore, among God's churches we boast about your perseverance and faith in all the persecutions and trials you are enduring (2 Thess. 1:3–4).

Imperfect though the church in Thessalonica may have been, Paul still begins his letter on a note of thanksgiving. There are errors to correct and people to rebuke, but these can wait. Pastoral wisdom and genuine affection both dictate that he begin with an outburst of gratitude.

True, he was also encouraged to begin this way by letter-writing convention. But as we have seen, Paul was no slave to convention. Though happy to conform to it, he never hesitated to break with it, or at least modify it, when occasion demanded. And we may be sure that he would not have begun by telling the Thessalonian Christians how thankful to God he was for them just for the sake of sticking to the rules. He does so, rather, because his heart is genuinely elated over all God has accomplished among them.

As was the case in 1 Thessalonians, the thanksgiving section of this letter has a clear beginning but no easily recognisable end. In fact, in the Greek text, verses 3–10 form a single unbroken sentence. What begins as a thanksgiving report merges into comment, encouragement and instruction on themes connected with it.

CONSTRAINED TO BE THANKFUL

Interestingly, the apostle introduces his thanksgiving report in a somewhat unusual way. He does not write, as he had in the first letter, 'We always thank God for all of you' (*1 Thess.* 1:2). Instead he tells them that he, Silas and Timothy feel a constant sense of obligation to thank God for them (v.3).

Some have taken this as an expression of reluctance and see in it the hint of a cooler tone to this letter. Paul has written one letter to the church, so it is said, and at least parts of that letter have not been heeded. Aspects of the church's life have in fact deteriorated rather than improved. And now he shows his displeasure in this rather un-natural and even stiff beginning.

But this is not necessarily the case, and certainly not what the effusive warmth of the following verses suggest Paul's attitude to have been. When the apostle speaks of being obliged to thank God for his readers, he is not implying that he is reluctant or feels forced against his will to do so. He is simply stating a fact. He and his fellow workers recognise that all the spiritual progress that has been made in the church in Thessalonica, all the many good virtues that abound in them, are the result of God's work in their hearts. They have not come about through their own skill or ingenuity, but through God's grace. Consequently, Paul, Silas and Timothy know that they ought always to thank God for them. It was only right for them to do so.

The act of thanking God can easily be under-emphasised in our worship. Its common neglect reflects our self-centredness. All too often we are more eager to receive new blessings than we are to ac-knowledge God's past and present goodness to us. The more clearly we appreciate our dependence upon him, the more we will find a thankful spirit come to dominate our lives and express itself in our prayers.

ABOUNDING FAITH AND LOVE

That for which Paul, Silas and Timothy were so thankful was the flourishing faith and love of the church (v.3).

Paul had been concerned about the faith of the Thessalonian Christians. It was not that they lacked faith altogether (*1 Thess.* 1:3), but their faith in the gospel had been put on trial (3:5) and was apparently defective at points (3:10). He desperately wanted to visit the church again, that he might supply what was lacking in this respect.

Somehow news had reached him that their faith was growing more and more (v.3). Like the lush foliage of a healthy and vigorous plant, it kept growing, presumably both in depth and in strength. This was indeed reason for thanks.

Similarly, their love toward each other was increasing, too. The congregation had been taught by God to love (*1 Thess.* 4:9), but Paul had wanted them to love more and more (4:10). This had been happening. Each of the members had been growing in love toward all the others. Love was welling up within them as a fountain and flowing outwards, embracing others in its streams. How could their founding missionaries be anything but overjoyed and thankful? With these two spiritual graces in such good heart, the foundations of the church were strong.

Faith and love, as we have seen, lie at the core of the Christian life. Faith brings us into fellowship with God and results in acts of love both to him and to other people (*Gal.* 5:6). Where faith and love are missing, true Christianity is also missing, or at best, ailing.

What is more, these are not fixed, static qualities. Both are consciously exercised and can grow. In the normal Christian life they do grow, and keep on growing. Faith does so as we learn more about God and come to trust him more completely. Love grows as our concern for others deepens and as we give ourselves more selflessly to them in costly service. This kind of progress should be our constant ambition.

Paul has mentioned faith and love, but not the third quality of the familiar triad, namely hope. Does this mean that the Thessalonian Christians were losing confidence in their future destiny? To say so is to read too much into this omission. This is not the only instance where Paul speaks of faith and love without mentioning hope (e.g., *1 Thess.* 3:6, *Gal.* 5:6, *Col.* 1:4). But more important, in the very next verse (v.4) Paul commends their perseverance. Since perseverance is the outcome of hope (*1 Thess.* 1:3), it seems clear that hope was not fading in the church. It was simply not at the forefront of Paul's mind when it came to thanking God for his work in the church.

GLAD BOASTING

So encouraged were Paul, Silas and Timothy with the spiritual progress of the Thessalonians that they were in the practice of singing
their praises to others (v.4).

As a rule, Paul was careful about boasting. He was especially careful that credit never be given to man when it was due to God (*1 Cor.*
1:31; 4:6–7). Yet he recognised that there was a place for speaking
to others about the great things God had done in the lives of people.
In writing to the church in Corinth, for example, he refers to the
outstanding generosity of the Macedonian churches (*2 Cor.* 8:1–7).
Significantly, he does not attribute their liberality to their own open-
handedness but to the grace God has given to them. And he does so
not to flatter the Macedonians, but to encourage the Corinthians to
be like them.

So in this case, Paul can speak of his boasting about the Thessalonians among God's churches – the other Christian congregations
with which he was in touch. He tells them of their perseverance and
faith in the midst of all their persecutions and trials. From the outset
the Thessalonian church had suffered fierce opposition, yet in spite
of that and the inevitable troubles it produced, they were showing
unwavering loyalty to Christ. God's grace was propping them up,
as it were. Unhesitatingly Paul tells others about this, using them as
an example to encourage and challenge those who may be showing
less courage.

But why should he bother telling the Thessalonians themselves
about this? Might it not make them big-headed? That certainly was
not Paul's intention. He tells them this to encourage them further.
Flattery is wrong, but so, too, is a failure to acknowledge God's grace
at work within people. There is a place for telling others of the
evident grace of God in their lives. Properly done, it can result in
enormous encouragement without creating the least taint of pride.

On this note of encouragement, then, Paul launches his second
letter to the Thessalonians. Assured of his good will toward them,
they will be the more ready to listen not only to his instruction, but
to his correction.

3

The Righteous Judgement of God

⁵All this is evidence that God's judgment is right, and as a result you will be counted worthy of the kingdom of God, for which you are suffering. ⁶God is just: He will pay back trouble to those who trouble you ⁷and give relief to you who are troubled, and to us as well (2 Thess. 1:5–7a).

On the surface it does not seem right that a just God can let his people suffer horrible injustice! If God is in control of all things, we reason, and if he is perfectly righteous, how can he let his children suffer totally unwarranted oppression and persecution?

This question has tormented many godly sufferers. Perhaps some in Thessalonica were grappling with it as well. Becoming a Christian and being persecuted went hand in hand in that city (*1 Thess.* 1:6). It must have seemed strange to some new believers that the true and living God they now served allowed them to suffer so unfairly at the hands of their wicked pagan neighbours. If he was the sovereign Lord, why did he not do something to stop it?

Paul seems to have questions like this in mind as he writes this second letter to the church. Its members were holding fast in spite of the opposition they were facing, and indeed, were growing immensely in their faith and love in the midst of it (vv.3–4). Nevertheless, it is not unlikely that at least some were troubled by the thought that God seemed less than fair in the way he was treating them.

The apostle wants to banish all such doubts, and he does so by helping his readers take a deeper view of their situation. If they could only see their sufferings in the right way, they would realise that God was at work in what was happening to them. Far from letting them down, he was in fact preparing them for glory.

GOD'S JUDGEMENT IS RIGHT

Having spoken so glowingly of their spiritual growth and perseverance under persecution, the apostle continues by saying that this situation which appears to be so unjust is to be understood as open evidence that God's judgement is indeed right (v.5).

How can Paul say this? The answer depends on what he means when he speaks of 'all this'. What does he have in mind? Is he referring to the persecutions and trials mentioned in the preceding verse? Or is he saying that the Thessalonians' flourishing spiritual growth and steadfast endurance under persecution is proof that God's judgement is right?

Some see Christian suffering itself as evidence of God's righteous judgement in action. Peter speaks of God preparing his people for glory by using trials and persecutions as a means of judging them in this world (*1 Pet.* 4:16–17). Judgement begins now for the household of God in order that they might escape it later. Understood this way, Paul would here be saying to the Thessalonians that their present sufferings are in fact a display of God's righteous judgement at work.

But this is not the only way, and perhaps not the most natural way, of understanding his words. Paul could also be speaking of the patience and prosperity of the Thessalonians in the midst of their sufferings. 'All this' served as a plain, visible token that God's judgement is right.

How, after all, can their growth in faith and love and their endurance be explained? These things were certainly not the result of unaided self-effort. They were the fruit of God's Spirit dwelling in them (*Gal.* 5:22). He had not abandoned them in their troubles, but was working mightily in them. And it was this fact that proved that God's judgement was indeed right. He was on their side, as it were, even though outwardly their circumstances seemed to suggest otherwise.

Paul says something similar to this to the Christians in Philippi. They, too, were suffering, and they are encouraged by the apostle to do so with firmness and without being frightened. 'Your fearless endurance', he says, 'will be a sign to your adversaries of their coming destruction but of your salvation' (*Phil.* 1:28). They will see your steadfastness and be compelled to recognise that God is with you and that they themselves are in the wrong. Your endurance will be an omen of their judgement, but of your final happiness.

This reminds us how careful we must be in interpreting the significance of suffering. Persecution and trial are not necessarily signs of God's displeasure. They are certainly never evidence of his injustice. He has many purposes in allowing his children to suffer.

As Christians we must never expect to have trouble-free lives. We must not become upset with God and begin to question his goodness when he allows unfair things to happen to us. What counts most is what God does in us and through us by means of our sufferings. We need to look below the surface and see his larger purposes in what we are enduring.

WORTHY OF THE KINGDOM

One of these larger purposes is preparation for the kingdom. Paul assures the Thessalonians that their sufferings have this end in view (v.5). The kingdom Paul has in mind is the future perfected kingdom of glory that will be fully realised at the end of this present age. While recognising that this kingdom had come in the person and ministry of Jesus, the apostle also understood that its coming, and our entrance into its glory, was also still in the future. And he has this joyous event in view as he writes here.

The Thessalonians are to understand that what is happening to them now will stand them in good stead when the time comes to inherit that kingdom. God's presence with them now can be taken as an assurance of his favour toward them then. But more than that, they can be sure that their patient endurance of persecution and trial for the sake of the kingdom will mean that they will be counted worthy of it when it comes.

It is not that their suffering will actually merit admission into the kingdom. Ultimately they are able to enter only through the merits of the Lord Jesus Christ. Paul is saying that their perseverance in suffering for the kingdom will be seen as evidence that they are those to whom the kingdom belongs. It will be proof of their faith in Christ and result in them being declared worthy of entering the glory that lies before them.

Tribulation and glory, suffering and the kingdom, are inseparably linked in the gospel. Jesus told his followers that persecution was inevitable (*John* 15:18) and that they were to rejoice when they suffered (*Luke* 6:23). In doing so, they were following the path of the prophets, and of their Master himself. Jesus suffered and then entered into glory (*Luke* 24:26). All who follow him necessarily share in some degree the same experience. Only those who have fellowship in his sufferings can anticipate fellowship with him in his glory (*Rom.* 8:17). Troubles litter the pathway leading to the kingdom (*Acts* 14:22).

PAYBACK TIME

The prospect of glory for kingdom sufferers rests on an unshakeable foundation, namely, that God is just (v.6). It belongs to the righteous character of God both to pay back trouble and to relieve those who are troubled (v.6). In grappling with this question of the justice of their sufferings, the Thessalonian Christians are to take comfort in knowing that God's final judgement will surely bring retribution upon those who have opposed them. God will pay back their troublers. As unpopular as the idea may be, there is such a thing as the retributive justice of God. He does repay evildoers for their wrongs.

For the present his people must suffer oppression, and they must suffer it patiently without personal retaliation (*Rom.* 12:19). It belongs to God to repay them for all the wrongs endured, and repay them he surely shall. One day their oppressors will reap what they have sown, because God is inflexibly just.

At that same time, those like the Thessalonian believers and the apostle and his helpers will at last know relief from their troubles. Acknowledged by the Lord as those blessed by his Father (*Matt.* 25:34), they will enter the kingdom prepared for them, a kingdom free from all evil and all suffering, a kingdom of perfect rest.

We must never allow undeserved suffering for Christ to give rise to hard thoughts about God. He knows what he is about, has a good purpose in all that happens to us, and will one day set everything right.

4

God's Dreadful Vengeance

⁷ᵇ This will happen when the Lord Jesus is revealed from heaven in blazing fire with his powerful angels. ⁸He will punish those who do not know God and do not obey the gospel of our Lord Jesus. ⁹They will be punished with everlasting destruction and shut out from the presence of the Lord and from the majesty of his power ¹⁰on the day he comes to be glorified in his holy people and to be marvelled at among all those who have believed. This includes you, because you believed our testimony to you (2 Thess. 1:7b–10).

Paul has been encouraging his readers by assuring them that their present persecution will come to an end. Although it may not seem like it to them, God's judgement is just, and he will one day set all wrongs right. He will pay back trouble to their oppressors and give them relief (vv.6–7a).

Having in this way alluded to a future retribution and deliverance, the apostle expands on this more fully in the verses which follow. He shows how God intends to accomplish these things and what it will mean both for those who are the objects of his judgement and for those who experience relief from persecution. In doing so he provides a vivid sketch of awesome future events that desperately need closer consideration today.

WHEN IT WILL TAKE PLACE

Paul mentions first when these coming events will happen. Punishment for the oppressors and relief for the oppressed will come about when the Lord Jesus is revealed from heaven (v.7b).

The idea of the Lord Jesus descending from heaven featured in Paul's first letter to the Thessalonian church. There the return of the Lord was discussed in connection with fears about Christians who had already died (*1 Thess.* 4:13–18). Here, however, his return is connected with the punishment of persecutors and the relief of Christian sufferers.

Correspondingly, the imagery Paul uses to describe this same event is strikingly different.

First, he speaks of the Lord Jesus being 'revealed' from heaven, not simply as making an 'official visit' (*parousia*) from heaven. This revelation is the unveiling of something previously hidden. The Lord himself has been the hidden observer of all that has happened to his people on earth. Suddenly he shall be unveiled both to them and to those who have been troubling them.

Secondly, his coming 'from heaven' is meant to suggest more than merely his place of origin. It points rather to his authority and power. Heaven is the dwelling place of God, and the Lord Jesus comes from God invested with divine authority to judge.

Thirdly, the Lord is revealed in blazing fire with his powerful angels. These images, drawn from Old Testament theophanies or appearances of God (*Exod.* 3:2; 19:18) reinforce the idea that the Lord Jesus comes with the full splendour and majesty of God himself. Fire, a common symbol of God's presence, speaks of Jesus' irresistible power as Judge. Nothing shall elude his scrutiny or escape his judgement. The angels of his power that accompany him witness to his royal authority to act in this role.

WHO IT WILL INVOLVE

One purpose of this unveiling will be to punish (v.8). The term 'punish' might equally be translated 'avenge', because Jesus comes to pay back trouble to those who tormented his followers (v.6). Many hesitate to associate the idea of vengeance with God because it is charged with images of unrestrained passion common to human revenge. God's vengeance, however, is untainted by vindictive passion. When he pays sinners back for their offences he never acts arbitrarily or in what we would call a spirit of revenge, but always in terms of strict justice. He repays people exactly what they deserve.

That Jesus is entrusted with punishing people is in keeping with his claim that the Father has given judgement into his hands (*John* 5:22). It also confirms his divine dignity. The Old Testament depicts the day of the Lord as the day when Yahweh judges people (*Zeph.* 1:7–9). The Lord Jesus is not just an exalted agent God uses for this task. He is God himself coming in judgement.

This judgement is destined for those who do not know God and do not obey the gospel. Elsewhere Paul insists that all people, both believers and unbelievers, shall have to appear before the judgement seat of Christ (*2 Cor.* 5:10). Here, however, he is not thinking of the general judgement itself, but of the punishment that God will pour on his enemies when the Lord Jesus appears from heaven.

It is unclear whether two different classes of people are in mind here, or one group described from two different angles. If the former, those who do not know God are most probably Gentiles, and those who do not obey the gospel of the Lord Jesus Christ, Jews. If, on the other hand, all unbelievers are in view, they are considered as those who have wilfully rejected the knowledge of God and spurned his mercy offered in the gospel.

While in this section Paul has persecutors at the forefront of his mind, he makes it clear that the Lord will inflict punishment on all unbelievers at his return.

WHAT IT WILL MEAN

How will the Lord Jesus punish people when he is revealed from heaven? The just penalty for oppressing Christians and for wilfully rejecting God and his gospel will be everlasting destruction (v.9). We have already encountered the idea of destruction in Paul's first letter to the Thessalonians (*1 Thess.* 5:3). There we noted that it does not refer to the complete dissolution of existence (annihilation), but to absolute loss and ruin. To suffer eternal destruction is to suffer the eternal loss of all that is truly worthwhile and meaningful. The final punishment of unbelievers may also entail other aspects of suffering (*Rev.* 20:15), but here Paul's emphasis is upon their tragic and irreversible loss.

That loss appears to be intimately connected with being permanently excluded from the Lord's presence (v.9). Again, we noted in

Paul's first letter to the Thessalonians that the climax of Christian hope and blessing is to be forever with the Lord (*1 Thess*. 4:17). Eternal life is to know God and to be with him in the presence of his glory (*John* 17:3, 24). Conversely, the greatest loss anyone can experience is to be deprived of that privilege. This is the fate that Jesus will assign to all who do not know and love him when he is revealed from heaven.

THE GLORY OF THE LORD

So far in this section Paul has emphasised God's vengeance. He is not totally forgetful, however, of other more positive events associated with the revelation of the Lord.

The day of the Lord will also be a day in which he is glorified in his people and marvelled at among believers (v.10). The same revelation that excites terror in one class of people will prompt adoration in another. Those who have suffered patiently for him, and indeed, all who believe the gospel, will gaze upon him with admiring wonder. His glory will far surpass anything they could have imagined and leave them struck with wonder.

Whether Paul also wants to include here the idea that believers will themselves share in the glory of Christ at his coming is uncertain. Paul says that Jesus will come to be glorified 'in' his holy people, not simply 'by' them. We know believers will be transformed into his image in that day, and that they will radiate his glory forever (*Phil.* 3:21). But all the same, here the focus is upon the Lord Jesus and the accolades he will receive from his people when he appears. While he comes to punish, he also comes to be praised.

The Thessalonians themselves can be confident of being among the adoring assembly that welcomes the Lord. Since it comprises all who have believed, it includes them (v.10). Their glad reception of the gospel (*1 Thess*.1:6) guaranteed their joyful future.

The significance of the events described in this section can hardly be overstated. They demand decision. In effect they tell us that nothing matters more than what happens to us when Jesus is revealed from heaven. Our destiny then hinges on our response to the gospel now. This should make us treasure that gospel ourselves and make it known to others.

5

Worthy of His Calling

¹¹With this in mind, we constantly pray for you, that our God may count you worthy of his calling, and that by his power he may fulfil every good purpose of yours and every act prompted by your faith. ¹²We pray this so that the name of our Lord Jesus may be glorified in you, and you in him, according to the grace of our God and the Lord Jesus Christ (2 Thess. 1:11–12).

Paul has left his readers on a high note at the end of his long thanksgiving sentence (vv.3–10). They have been praised for their progress in faith and love and assured that God will one day bring their sufferings to an end. When the Lord Jesus is revealed from heaven he will punish their oppressors with eternal destruction but welcome the believers into his presence.

Confident as he is that the Thessalonian Christians will share in the blessings of that day (v.10), the apostle nevertheless does not relax his concern for them. Certainty of being in the presence of Christ in the future does not breed complacency in the present. It rather acts as a powerful incentive to holiness (*1 John* 3:3). Those eager to share in Jesus' glory then make themselves ready for it now.

This outlook prompts the apostle and his helpers to keep on praying for their friends in Thessalonica. They not only thank the Lord for what he has done in the lives of these former pagans (1:3), but they pray that the work begun in them will continue till the day of the Lord (*Phil.* 1:6)

COUNTED WORTHY

Paul is here not so much inserting an actual prayer into his letter as assuring his readers that he and his colleagues do pray constantly for them (v.11). Reflection on the Thessalonians' future participation in the glory of Christ inspires the missionaries to pray for them.

In particular they pray that God may count them worthy of his calling (v.11). As he mentions this, Paul still has in mind the Lord's appearing. He and his colleagues want the Thessalonians to be able to appear before God in a condition that will win his approval. God has called them to his kingdom and glory (*1 Thess.* 2:12), and the apostle longs that they may be counted worthy of such a calling when they stand before him. He has already expressed this wish for them in his first letter in terms of them appearing holy and blameless before God at the coming of the Lord with all his holy ones (*1 Thess.* 3:13). He is repeating that same desire here.

We have already noted that this thought of being approved by God when we appear before him is not to be confused with earning salvation by works. Our salvation is grounded in God's election and subsequent calling to faith in Christ through the gospel. We enter the kingdom because God has chosen us to be his children and destined us to be his heirs. Salvation is of God from beginning to end. Paul is not suggesting anything else at this point. He is simply saying that when the time comes for us to enter the glory of the kingdom, we must aim to be those God will count worthy of it. Our lives should be consistent with our calling.

POWER FOR LIFE

But how can we live such lives? The rest of Paul's prayer gives us the answer. Paul's readers will be counted worthy of their calling as God works in them powerfully to fulfil their good purposes and their acts prompted by faith (v.11).

The Thessalonians already have a living, active faith. They have good purposes springing up in their hearts and are stimulated by their faith to perform practical acts (*1 Thess.* 1:3). These things, of course, are ultimately due to God's work within them. It is God who works in us 'to will and act according to his good purpose' (*Phil.* 2:13).

But God's work in us calls for a response on our part. Through his Spirit living in us he implants good purposes within our hearts as we respond in faith to his word. But these purposes and their associated desires and plans must be carried into practical action.

At this point, we need to look beyond ourselves to God in prayer for his enabling to do even the things that he has already made us want to do.

This is exactly the point of Paul's prayer for the Thessalonian Christians. He knows they need the power of God to work out their faith in acts of practical service. And since prayer is the channel God has provided for obtaining that power, the apostle and his fellow missionaries pray constantly that God would supply what their converts need. Only through his enabling will they be able to do the things that will make them worthy of their calling.

GLORIFICATION

The aim of all of this is not the final happiness of the Thessalonian Christians, so much as the glory of the Lord Jesus (v.12). The apostle never loses sight of the pre-eminence of the Lord Jesus Christ. As important as it may be for Christians to be commended by God and counted worthy of the kingdom, the point of their living holy lives is not firstly for their own sake, but rather for the glory of the Lord Jesus when he returns.

We have noted (v.10) that the Lord will return to be 'glorified in his holy people'. Paul is alluding to that same idea here. He seems to be referring to the way in which holy, fruit-filled lives will be to Jesus' honour when he returns. They will glorify his name because they are the product of his work as Saviour and Lord. His death and his resurrection life are the only reason that we will be able to stand in God's presence and have any works of worth to show. The apostle has in his mind the picture of his readers, many of whom were once crass pagans, standing before the Lord as transformed people, trophies of his own redeeming grace. And it is the glory of the Lord displayed in such lives that spurs Paul to pray for them.

But that is not all. He knows that it will be not only the Lord who will be glorified at his appearing, but also 'you in him' (v.12). When he comes it will be patently clear that believers belong to him. Already through his transforming grace they have become like him, and through his enabling they have lived worthy of their calling. Then they will have the joy of inheriting with him the kingdom prepared by the Father.

ALL OF GRACE

Not for a moment, however, will that be considered the reward of their own efforts. All will freely admit that it is according to the grace of our God and the Lord Jesus Christ (v.12). God's grace, his unde-served favour in action, is the source of every spiritual blessing. We recognise that grace lies at the root of our conversion. But in the future we will also recognise that grace is the only explanation for our glorification. We will then see more clearly than ever that we have been called by grace, lived by grace, and finally exalted with the Lord Jesus Christ by grace.

Through the eternity to come we will never tire of boasting that we are debtors to the grace of our God and the Lord Jesus Christ.

6

No Need For Alarm

[1]Concerning the coming of our Lord Jesus Christ and our being gathered to him, we ask you, brothers, [2]not to become easily unsettled or alarmed by some prophecy, report or letter supposed to have come from us, saying that the day of the Lord has already come. [3]Don't let anyone deceive you in any way, for that day will not come until the rebellion occurs and the man of lawlessness is revealed, the man doomed to destruction (2 Thess. 2:1–3).

The second chapter introduces a new section of the letter. While not unrelated to what has preceded, it nevertheless addresses a fresh concern, one that evidently lies at the heart of Paul's purpose in writing. Mistaken notions regarding the nearness of the Lord's return had created problems in the church in Thessalonica. They threatened the stability of the faint-hearted and added weight to the no-work policy of the idle. They needed settling quickly.

Paul's response to this problem presents us with one of the most obscure and difficult passages in his writings. In part the difficulty arises from the fact that we do not know what Paul assumes his readers know. He is not introducing new information here, but reminding the Thessalonians of what he taught them while with them (v.5). We have no record of that oral instruction and have to admit that, at points, the apostle's readers would have understood clearly what we discern at best tentatively.

Our disadvantage in this respect means that we must live with a measure of uncertainty. We must also keep in bounds the curiosity aroused by the sensational character of the subject matter. As exciting as it might be to know the identity of Paul's 'man of lawlessness' and the time of his revelation, we cannot pinpoint these. Nor was it Paul's intention that his original readers should, either. His purpose was to correct enthusiasts and encourage the fearful. His words still do that effectively today.

THE PROBLEM

Paul begins by identifying the problem area. It concerns the coming of our Lord Jesus Christ and our being gathered to him (v.1).

At first glance this may appear to be the same topic that absorbed his attention in the opening chapter. In one sense it is, but in another it is not. True, the apostle has been writing about the revelation or the unveiling of the Lord Jesus (1:7–10). But that was in connection with punishing those who were persecuting the Thessalonian Christians. Here, however, his subject is the coming (*parousia*) of the Lord Jesus and the gathering of his people to him. While this apparently refers to the same event, it is looked at from a different angle. Paul is thinking here not so much of the revelation of the Lord as the Judge of the wicked, but of his coming as the Saviour of his people.

For Christians, the coming of the Lord is always to be associated with their being gathered to him. This expression has roots in the messianic hope of the Old Testament. The prophets pointed to the day when the Lord would assemble his scattered people in their own land (*Isa.* 52:12, *Zech.* 2:6). Paul sees this being fulfilled in the final gathering of his people with the Messiah at the *parousia*. It is then that God will come and dwell with his people forever, and they will enter into the full blessing of their calling.

Paul makes a strong plea in regard to this subject. He does not want the church to become unsettled or alarmed by rumours they might hear about the Lord's return (v.2). Apparently this had been happening. At least a section of the congregation had been caught up in a spirit of nervous excitement and was acting irrationally and irresponsibly. In spite of all Paul had taught them about the second coming, they were being tossed about like waves in the wind and in danger of losing their moorings. Anxiety and its resulting confusion was the pastoral problem he needed to resolve.

ITS ALLEGED SOURCE

It was of special concern to him because of its supposed source. It evidently grew out of some prophecy, report, or letter alleged to have come from the apostle and his helpers (v.2). News had somehow reached the Thessalonians that Paul was teaching the immediate nearness of the return of the Lord Jesus.

The claim being made was that the day of the Lord had already come. In this context, the expression 'the day of the Lord' does not refer to a twenty-four hour day, or to the actual visible appearing of the Lord Jesus. It refers to the larger complex of events associated with the final appearing of the Lord. Taken together, these events, including the climactic appearance of the Judge himself, make up 'the day of the Lord'. And these, it was being said on Paul's authority, had begun to come to pass. Clearly, the return of the Lord Jesus was immediately at hand.

Naturally news of this sort would create a stir, especially among those who feared they were not ready to meet the Lord. Paul, however, tells his readers they are not to let themselves be tossed about by such reports; they must not let anyone deceive them in this matter (v.3).

Warnings against deception are often linked with predictions of the return of the Lord Jesus. The spectacular character of that event makes it prone to counterfeit claims. Jesus warned of people who would deceive many by claiming to be the Christ (*Mark* 13:5) or by saying that he had appeared in this place or that (*Matt.* 24:26). His disciples were to be on guard against such delusions, precisely the counsel Paul gives the Thessalonian Christians here.

ITS ANTIDOTE

But how can Paul be so sure that the day of the Lord has not come? An answer is close at hand. Two related events must occur before the day of the Lord comes (v.3).

The first is the rebellion. The fact that Paul does not further qualify this apostasy indicates that his readers already know about it. They had almost certainly heard of Jesus' teaching about conditions in the end times. He had spoken of coming days in which opposition to God would grow and wickedness and immorality abound (*Matt.* 24:12). This would be associated with increased warfare between nations, the rise of false prophets and teachers who would seek to lead people astray (*Mark* 13:7, 22), and heightened persecution of the church (*Mark* 13:9–13). Paul probably has this common view of last times apostasy in mind here when he speaks of the rebellion. He is more likely to be thinking of this general condition of mankind than, as some prefer, a widespread defection from the church itself.

The second event that must come to pass before the return of the Lord is the revelation of the man of lawlessness (v.3). This is the only reference Paul makes in his writings to such a figure. He is the apostle's equivalent to John's antichrist (*1 John* 2:18; 4:3).

He is called here the 'man of lawlessness' because of his complete opposition to God. He is the one who embodies in its highest form man's rebellion against God. He rejects not only the Old Testament law, but all that claims to belong to God and be of God. He wants to claim divine rights for himself (v.4). Although a man, and not Satan or some superhuman being, he is nevertheless the arch-agent of the devil.

The apostle says that this figure has yet to be revealed. This may be taken to mean that Paul thought he was already in existence but still waiting disclosure, though it is more likely that he has in mind a future appearance at a properly appointed time.

One more fact is stated about him. He is also described as 'the man doomed to destruction'. Paul will have more to say about his final ruin (v.8) but cannot resist labelling him from the outset as a doomed foe. His destiny is already fixed and is inescapably certain. Christians need not be intimidated by the thought of him.

7

The Man of Lawlessness

*⁴He will oppose and will exalt himself over everything that is
called God or is worshipped, so that he sets himself up in God's
temple, proclaiming himself to be God.*

*⁵Don't you remember that when I was with you I used to
tell you these things? ⁶And now you know what is holding him
back, so that he may be revealed at the proper time. ⁷For the
secret power of lawlessness is already at work; but the one who
now holds it back will continue to do so till he is taken out of
the way. ⁸And then the lawless one will be revealed, whom the
Lord Jesus will overthrow with the breath of his mouth and
destroy by the splendour of his coming* (2 Thess. 2:4–8).

Few characters in the Bible excite more curiosity than the man
of lawlessness. Paul introduces this figure to his Thessalonian
readers in an attempt to allay their fears about the onset of the day
of the Lord. Rumours had reached them, supposedly originating
with the apostle himself, to the effect this day had already come (v.2).
In countering this error, Paul insists that before the day of the Lord
can come, certain events must take place. There must be a great
rebellion culminating in the revelation of the man of lawlessness.

Having in this way drawn attention to the coming arch-rebel, the
apostle expands briefly on his activity, his present delay, and his
certain destruction.

HIS ACTIVITY

The central characteristic of the man of lawlessness is his total
rejection of authority, and especially of all that claims to be God (v.4).

The militant character of his opposition is foremost in Paul's mind here. This will presumably be expressed not only in a vehement rejection of all human religions, but also in the aggressive repression of every act of worship among people. His coming will mark an era of intensified persecution for all devout worshippers.

In addition, he will exalt himself over every confessed deity. He will be bent upon setting himself in a position above God. At heart he is an avowed opponent of all authority except his own. He will defy all existing law, be that moral, religious or civil, in order to assume a place of unrivalled supremacy himself.

He will do this by taking to himself the honour due to God alone. For one thing, he will set himself up in God's temple (v.4). Whether this means the literal occupation of a physical temple, or assuming authority in the church as the new temple of God (*Eph.* 1:21,22), is not immediately apparent from Paul's words. It is perhaps best to take the words in a metaphorical sense. To set oneself up in the temple of God is to invade the dwelling place of God and assume the rights of God. What is clear is that the man of lawlessness will usurp the authority and homage due to God alone.

Along with that, he will actually claim to be God (v.4). He will set himself up as the unrivalled object of homage and source of authority. Worship once devoted to other gods must now be directed to him. This will be the supreme act of his spiritual rebellion, the final revelation of the apostasy and blasphemy of the ages.

HIS DELAY

Apparently this was information Paul's readers should already have known (v.5). The emergence of a great antichristian figure at the end of history had featured in Paul's preaching to them. It would seem, given John's parallel mention of a coming antichrist (*1 John* 2:18), that this was a common element in the preaching of all the apostles.

The Thessalonian Christians knew not only about this coming usurper, but also about what was holding him back (v.6). The secret power of lawlessness already at work in the world (v.7) was being held back by a restraint that would remain until God's time for the revelation of the man of lawlessness. At that time the hindrance would be taken out of the way and its full power revealed openly, concentrated in the form of this figure about which the apostle has been talking (v.8).

We can only speculate about the identity of this restraining force or influence. Since the Thessalonians learned about it through Paul's oral teaching rather than through his letters, we must content ourselves with our lesser understanding on this point. Credible theories have been offered to explain its nature. Two of these seem to the present writer to have most merit:

Some suggest that the restraint is essentially an influence for good that may be embodied in either a person or a principle. Those holding to this interpretation generally see the law and order associated with good government and just rulers as the restraint holding back the man of lawlessness.

Others connect the restraint more directly with God himself and with his purpose that the gospel should be preached throughout the earth before the end comes (*2 Pet.* 3:9, *Matt.* 24:14). Until that purpose is fully accomplished, God, perhaps through the mediation of heavenly beings, restrains the development of lawlessness.

The result of this restraining influence, whatever its nature, is that for the moment, lawlessness operates as a secret power (v.7). While not totally hidden, it nevertheless cannot flourish openly. It bubbles beneath the surface awaiting its time to erupt and envelop the earth in evil. That eruption will occur at God's appointed time, when that which currently holds back its spread is taken out of the way.

Paul does not write these things to stimulate the curiosity of the Thessalonians, nor, for that matter, ours. He is not providing a timetable of future events for end-time speculators but writing as a pastor to settle a disturbed flock. He wants his readers to know that certain future events must take place before the Lord returns. Lawlessness, culminating in the revelation of the man of lawlessness, must first of all increase. But even that, they must know, is also in the hand of God. Powerful though the coming one might be, the Lord himself yet remains in supreme control.

HIS DESTRUCTION

Further details of this powerful figure and his activities remain tantalisingly obscure. Most of us would like to know when he will come, what he will look like, where he will base his activities, and how long he will dominate. But these things are hidden from us. The apostle does not want us to develop an absorbing fascination with him.

What he does want us to know, along with the certainty of his appearance as a precursor to the day of the Lord, is that he will be utterly overthrown and destroyed by the Lord Jesus Christ (v.8). His ruin is presented as a decisive event connected to the coming of the Lord Jesus. As mentioned, we have no idea how long he will be allowed to parade his arrogance before this will happen. But when it does, there will be no protracted conflict. The man of lawlessness will be rendered powerless, in a moment of divine triumph.

The Lord Jesus will overthrow him with the 'breath of his mouth'. Elsewhere the conquering Lord is pictured with a sword coming out of his mouth (*Rev.* 2:16; 19:15). The all-prevailing word of the Lord will forever silence the hollow claims of this arrogant blasphemer (v.4; *Isa.* 11:4).

He will also be overwhelmed by the 'splendour' of Jesus' coming. Isaiah, Ezekiel, Daniel, Paul and John, all holy servants of the Lord, were unable to stand in the presence of God's revealed majesty. How much less will the one who has defied God and usurped his prerogatives! The appearance of the Lord in the splendour of his heavenly glory will render his arch-adversary powerless.

What stability and comfort these words supply! They warn against premature panic concerning the day of the Lord and assure of the ultimate triumph of Christ in the end. The man of lawlessness will have his day, but he will also meet his doom.

8

Deception and Condemnation

⁹The coming of the lawless one will be in accordance with the work of Satan displayed in all kinds of counterfeit miracles, signs and wonders, ¹⁰and in every sort of evil that deceives those who are perishing. They perish because they refused to love the truth and so be saved. ¹¹For this reason God sends them a powerful delusion so that they will believe the lie ¹²and so that all will be condemned who have not believed the truth but have delighted in wickedness (2 Thess. 2:9–12).

Paul has sketched three major events in God's programme for the future. He has spoken of a rebellion, of the revelation of the man of lawlessness, and of the coming of the Lord Jesus. His Thessalonian readers need not fear that the day of the Lord has come until they see the first two events in this drama unfold.

The man of lawlessness remains the focus of the verses before us. Although the apostle has spoken of his destruction at the coming of the Lord (v.8), he continues to describe the nature and consequences of his activity during the period of his power. What he says helps us to understand the deeper processes at work behind the awesome events that will usher in the end of the age.

ANOTHER PAROUSIA

The first thing that Paul mentions about the coming of the lawless one is that it will be in accordance with the work of Satan (v.9).

Like the Lord Jesus, the man of lawlessness is said to have a coming, or *parousia*. Paul almost certainly wants his readers to recognise this parallel. He wants them to understand that Satan will attempt to deceive people at the end of the world with a blasphemous substitute for Jesus. The climax of God's saving plan is marked by the *parousia* of Jesus. The culmination of Satan's opposition to God will be the *parousia* of the man of lawlessness.

Throughout the Scriptures Satan appears as a liar (*John* 8:44), the master of masquerade (*2 Cor.* 11:14). The coming of the lawless one will be his attempt to counterfeit the appearing of the Lord Jesus Christ.

His coming will be correspondingly impressive. Though a man, the lawless one will be empowered with superhuman abilities. He will come anointed with the might of his master. Just as Jesus will come in the glory of his Father, the antichrist will come in accordance with the work of Satan. The active power of Satan will be at work in him fitting him to be his agent in the great rebellion.

COUNTERFEIT SIGNS

Satan's power will show itself in the great diversity of counterfeit miracles, signs and wonders (v.9) that his underling will work.

Miracles, signs and wonders were the hallmark of Jesus' ministry on earth. They authenticated his claim to be the Son of God from heaven. The man of lawlessness, at the instigation of Satan, will copy these works to make people worship him as God.

His miracles will be genuine in the sense that they will not be mere visual delusions or tricks. It is quite within Satan's power to make supernatural things happen. Their counterfeit character lies in their source and intention. They aim to make people think that God is at work, but in fact, their purpose is to make people believe that the one who performs them is God. In that sense they are not genuine signs, but lies.

Deception lies at the root of Satan's design. He will stop at nothing to delude people. Every sort of evil that deceives will be the under-lying motto of his actions. Evil, or unrighteousness, is the fountain of his actions. Deception is the grand result that he seeks.

UNBELIEVERS DECEIVED

Not everyone will fall prey to these false signs, however, but only those people already on the path to eternal death (v.10). They are perishing because they refused to love the truth and so be saved. Apparently Paul is referring to people who have rejected the gospel. They have heard the truth – which in Paul's terminology is essentially the same as the gospel – and been urged to embrace it. However, they have wilfully refused to receive it as the means of their salvation. As a result, they are on the road to destruction.

Their problem in the final analysis is one of the heart rather than of the intellect. They do not receive the truth because they do not love it. The gospel might make sense to them and even seem to be logically convincing. But they will not respond to it because they have no taste for it. They prefer the flavour of evil. Consequently, they are ripe for the delusions of the man of lawlessness.

A POWERFUL DELUSION

But there is more to their fall than the craft of this arch-deceiver. God, too, is active in this end-time process. He is no mere bystander permitting the man of lawlessness to hold sway over the lives of people. He is in control of the whole process of false miracles and delusion, and he uses it for his own ends.

Specifically, he uses the deception of the man of lawlessness as a means of hardening those who have rejected the gospel. In what seems to us a startling declaration, Paul says that God actually sends a powerful delusion upon those who refuse to love the truth, so that they will believe the lie (v.11). In some way he disposes them to hear and believe the errors of Satan as spread by the lawless one. They have rejected the truth, and because of this, God abandons them to the lie.

Paul describes an exact parallel to this process elsewhere (*Rom.* 1:18–32). There he tells of what happens to people who wilfully reject God's self-revelation in nature. When men and women blot the God of creation from their minds and choose instead to worship idols, he gives them up to their corrupt desires and empty minds to become even more deeply immersed in acts that will finally condemn them (vv.24, 28). He judges people for their unbelief by abandoning them to outlandish forms of sin. If they will not have him, he will let them go their way and reap the full consequences of their folly.

In doing so, God is not the author of their sin. He removes restraints and sends delusions in ways that make men and women more disposed to sin themselves. They plunge more deeply into sin and fall prey more quickly to deception as a result of God's judgement upon them. But their actions are their own, and their judgement is deserved. God cannot be blamed for their acts or for their consequences.

Nor must we imagine that in acting this way God is merely outsmarting Satan. Rather, he is using him. It is wrong to think of God and the devil locked in a conflict that God only just manages to win. He is totally in control of his adversary and is able to use him to accomplish his own plans at any point.

CONDEMNATION

In this particular case, God uses Satan and the man of lawlessness so that all who have not believed the truth but have enjoyed wickedness will be condemned (v.12). They have rejected the truth not because it is beyond their comprehension or because it is illogical. They have done so because they have loved wickedness. And for that, they are justly punished. They would have been condemned anyway for their unbelief and sins, but by following the man of lawlessness they will be counted even more worthy of that sentence and reap the heavier punishment.

Scorning God's truth is a serious matter. In mercy and love he provides sinners with a gospel of reconciliation through Christ. If they receive it, they receive life. But if they reject it, there remains 'no sacrifice for sins' but only 'a fearful expectation of judgement and of raging fire that will consume the enemies of God' (*Heb.* 10: 26–27).

9

Assured of Glory

¹³But we ought always to thank God for you, brothers loved by the Lord, because from the beginning God chose you to be saved through the sanctifying work of the Spirit and through belief in the truth. ¹⁴He called you to this through our gospel, that you might share in the glory of our Lord Jesus Christ. ¹⁵So then, brothers, stand firm and hold to the teachings we passed on to you, whether by word of mouth or by letter.

¹⁶May our Lord Jesus Christ himself and God our Father, who loved us and by his grace gave us eternal encouragement and good hope, ¹⁷encourage your hearts and strengthen you in every good deed and word (2 Thess. 2:13–17).

Paul's description of the man of lawlessness and his awesome powers has been solemn to the point of being frightening. Though intended to comfort his friends in Thessalonica, it could not help but stir up their apprehensions as well. The timid among them especially would probably be thrown into deeper anxiety about the future. Would they be able to withstand the satanic workings of this deceiver? Would they end up being hardened with a spirit of delusion and finally condemned?

To counter such fears, the apostle ends this section on an assuring note. Aware that multitudes will fall prey to the wiles of the man of lawlessness and suffer doom, he is confident that this will not be the fate of his readers. On the contrary, whenever he thinks of them in connection with coming events, he cannot restrain himself from thanking God. His grace to the Thessalonian Christians means that they will not be condemned, but saved in the day of his wrath (*1 Thess.* 1:10).

THANKSGIVING

This confidence provided another reason why Paul and his associates felt they ought always to thank God for their brothers in Thessalonica (v.13). Earlier we noted that they felt it only proper to thank God on account of the progress the church had made in its spiritual life (1:3). Here the apostle says they feel that same inner compulsion as they reflect on God's grace in securing their salvation.

They know that their friends will not be condemned because they are loved and chosen by God to be saved (v.13). Ultimately their security rests not on anything they have done, but upon what God has done for them. Throughout his letters Paul traces salvation to its source in the good pleasure and sovereign will of God (*Eph.* 1:4–11, *2 Tim.* 1:9). It stems from his loving act of choosing sinners to be saved quite apart from their merits or foreseen actions. The infallible character of that choice is what makes the salvation of the elect so certain and the cause for such deep humility and joy on their part.

That is not to say, however, that the salvation of the elect is guaranteed apart from anything happening to them. Paul speaks here of his friends as those chosen to be saved through the sanctifying work of the Spirit and through belief in the truth. God saves his chosen people through a process of making them holy believers!

The apostle probably still has in mind the character of those deluded by the man of lawlessness. Their lives are marked by rejection of the truth on the one hand, and by love of wickedness on the other (v.12). God's plan for his people entails a total reversal of that condition. He means them to be lovers of the truth and rejecters of wickedness.

This great reversal had taken place in the Thessalonians as a result of the ministry of Paul, Silas and Timothy among them (v.14). Though God's plan of salvation is anchored in eternity, it is activated through the preaching of the gospel. Those whom he predestines he also calls through the gospel entrusted to men (*Rom.* 8:28–30). They hear the gospel, believe it through the power of the Holy Spirit, and turn from their evil ways. This is exactly what had happened in Thessalonica (*1 Thess.* 1:5–10).

We come to know that God has chosen us in this same way. We cannot read his mind and discover his plans directly. But we can know how we have responded to the gospel. If we have heard and believed the gospel and experienced the transforming work of the Holy Spirit in our lives, then we have good grounds to believe that we are God's elect people.

What makes this so glorious is the end that God has in view in saving his people. He does so not only that they might escape condemnation but that they might share in the glory of our Lord Jesus Christ (v.16). They are destined not only for deliverance but also for glorification! No wonder Paul and his fellow missionaries felt so constrained to thank God every time they thought of the Thessalonians.

INSTRUCTION

Having assured his readers of their destiny in the day of the Lord, the apostle exhorts them to live appropriately. Have they been chosen by God to be saved rather than condemned? Then, they must stand firm and hold to the teachings they were given (v.15).

This entire section of his letter had been prompted by false reports that the day of the Lord had come (v.2). These had alarmed at least some of the congregation and resulted in a state of unsettledness. How fitting, then, having instructed them so fully about the events that must precede the coming of the Lord and assured them of their safety in that day, that Paul should encourage them to stand firm. They had no cause at all to be so tossed about in this matter.

What he had written should also have renewed their confidence in the teachings that had originally been delivered to them. True, Paul and his associates had not been able to stay long in Thessalonica. Nevertheless, they had been there long enough and subsequently written fully enough for them to have received the body of apostolic teaching that formed the foundation of all the churches.

This body of truth, known as the apostolic tradition (Greek *paradosis*), was to serve as the authoritative reference point for their life. They were to hold to those teachings that had been passed on to them, whether by word of mouth or letter, and not allow themselves to be tossed about by forged letters or rumours.

That same apostolic tradition has been recorded in the New Testament scriptures and remains the standard for church and

Christian life today. It contains all that we need to know about God, about salvation, about the future, and about how to live. Endless trouble always results when we, like the Thessalonians, listen to anything else that claims to be God's message to us.

PRAYER

Fittingly, Paul closes this section of his letter with a prayer. Mistaken conceptions about the coming of the day of the Lord have been put to rest and his readers comforted and instructed regarding the way they are to approach the future. He has told them all they need to know, but he is aware at the same time that they need the power of God to translate this into daily reality. Hence, he prays for them.

The first part of his prayer is an extended description of the object of his prayer. It is to our Lord Jesus Christ himself and God our Father (v.16). Both the Father and Son are looked to for help. The church exists in God our Father and the Lord Jesus Christ (1:1) and properly looks to both for grace and help in times of need.

Paul refers to the object of his prayer, the Lord Jesus and the Father, as the one who loved us and by his grace gave us eternal encouragement and good hope (v.16). His previous discussion centred on God's love in choosing and calling and glorifying them. Out of his grace he has also given them encouragement that extends beyond time, as well as a good hope of glorious things to come. That is the God to whom he looks on their behalf.

His prayer for them resembles the one offered in his first letter (*1 Thess.* 3:13). Essentially it is a prayer for inner strength. He asks that God would encourage and strengthen them (v.17). He knows that their greatest need is for inner stability, for unwavering faith and constant hope and love, as they wait for the coming of the Lord. Perhaps God would use even the very words he has been writing to inspire and encourage them inwardly by the Holy Spirit (*Eph.* 3:16).

But inward resilience is not all he asks for. As well as steadfast, he wants the Christians in Thessalonica to be productive as they wait for the Lord. He knows that as they live in the Father and in his Son they will be filled with good purposes and be prompted to act out of faith (1:11). So here he prays that they would be strengthened in every good deed and word (v.17). He wants them to know God's power to perform those deeds and speak those words that belong to the Christian's life of loving service and gospel witness.

Inner strength is the basis of Christian stability. No amount of activity or positive thinking can compensate for the resolve and energy that God creates in the heart through his word and Spirit. We can only hope to withstand outward pressures as we constantly experience inward renewal.

IO

Praying for the Gospel

> *¹Finally, brothers, pray for us that the message of the Lord may spread rapidly and be honoured, just as it was with you. ²And pray that we may be delivered from wicked and evil men, for not everyone has faith. ³But the Lord is faithful, and he will strengthen and protect you from the evil one* (2 Thess. 3:1–3).

The expression 'finally, brothers' usually signals the beginning of a new section in Paul's letters. It does not necessarily mean that the apostle has come to the last thing he wants to say, but it commonly indicates that he has either finished, or is about to finish, dealing with the most important issues that prompted him to write.

In this letter so far, Paul has addressed two major concerns troubling the Thessalonian Christians. He has assured them that God has not forgotten them in their sufferings (1:3–12), and he has calmed their fears regarding the coming of the day of the Lord (2:1–17). One matter remains for him to write about: the problem of persistent refusal by some members of the church to work as they wait for the Lord to come.

But before taking up this issue, Paul makes a request of his fellow believers. He, Silas and Timothy are facing their own difficulties in Corinth and very much need the prayer fellowship of their friends in Thessalonica. 'Pray for us,' he writes (v.1).

RAPID SPREAD OF THE GOSPEL

One might expect that after making this plea the apostle would go on to specify some particular personal need that he and his companions had. That, after all, is the shape our prayer requests typically take.

Not so Paul. He does not ask his readers to pray for his safety or for sufficient funds to support the mission in Corinth. He wants them to pray for the advance of the Lord's message (v.1). His concern is not so much for the well-being of its messengers, but for the success of the gospel. What happens to him personally does not really matter to the apostle (*Acts* 20:24). He lived for the advance of the Lord's message. This single, self-denying passion lay behind his tireless work and colossal achievements. It remains the condition of effective gospel ministry still today.

In asking the believers to pray that the word of the Lord would spread rapidly and be honoured, Paul speaks almost as though the gospel had a life of its own. He wants it to run like a swift athlete through the world and be received as a victorious hero wherever it goes.

That apparently had happened in Thessalonica. The message of the Lord had come with power and been gladly received by some of the Jews and a great number of God-fearing Greeks (*Acts* 17:4, *1 Thess*. 1:4–5). Although there had been opposition, the gospel had nevertheless spread rapidly.

Paul's words suggest that the situation was somewhat different in Corinth, the scene of his present missionary work. The word of the Lord was not spreading as swiftly there as it had farther north in Macedonia. Luke, in his account of the mission in Corinth (*Acts* 18:5–17), tells of the strong opposition Paul encountered in that city from unbelieving Jews. They made his task very difficult and discouraging, a fact probably reflected in this plea to the Thessalonians for continuing prayer.

Paul realised, as we must, that only the Holy Spirit makes gospel preaching effective (*1 Cor*. 2:4–5). Prayer and preaching must be intertwined (*Acts* 6:4) if the word of the Lord is to spread rapidly and be honoured among men.

PROTECTION FROM EVIL MEN

Closely connected with this first request is a second for deliverance from wicked and evil men (v.2). When making this request, Paul is probably not thinking of wicked men in general, but of those who specifically reject and oppose the gospel. His preaching typically had a twofold effect upon people (*2 Cor.* 2:16). Some responded with joyful acceptance and became imitators of his way of life. Others rejected what he had to say and became his implacable enemies and opponents of the gospel. It is almost certainly this latter group that he refers to here, for their behaviour is related to the fact that not everyone has faith (v.2).

They are described as 'wicked and evil men' on account of the viciousness of their actions. Their thoughts and passions are corrupt and their dealings with other people destructive. They do not let the gospel pass them by with an indifferent shake of the head, but oppose it and its messengers violently.

It was for deliverance from such men that Paul asked the Thessalonians to pray. Once more, his concern was not primarily for his own safety but for the advance of the gospel. The people in view – in this case probably unbelieving Jews – were ready to do anything to rid the city of the pestilent message of the cross. Only as the missionaries were delivered from them was there any hope of the word of the Lord continuing to spread in Corinth and beyond.

Gospel preaching still arouses hostility today. In praying for evangelism and missionary enterprises we must ask not only for power for the message, but also for the protection of the messengers.

THE FAITHFUL LORD

Real as the threat posed by unbelievers might be, it does not dominate the apostle in a way that makes him cower and lose confidence. On the contrary, he knows that the Lord is faithful (v.3) and will never forsake those who put their trust in him (*Psa.* 9:10).

This confidence the apostle wants his readers to share fully in their own situation. While seeking their help for his own special needs as a preacher of the gospel, he does not forget their struggles. He knows that they, too, face the hostility of men and women who do not have faith, and that they need to share in the comfort that comes from knowing the Lord's faithfulness.

In that regard, he assures them that the Lord Jesus will strengthen and protect them from the evil one (v.3). Our translation suggests that their trouble comes from a personal source of evil, the devil. This wicked adversary lies behind every expression of opposition to the gospel and godly living. We need to be reminded constantly of his restless activity. To underestimate his craft and power is a tragic mistake.

The Lord Jesus, however, is able to strengthen and protect against every form of evil that the devil contrives against us. The Lord is able to supply the inward discernment, resolution and vigilance that enable us to overcome Satan's attacks (*Eph.* 6:10–17). More than that, he is able to stand guard over us, protecting us from assaults beyond our strength to endure (*1 Cor.* 10:13). In this he is our totally faithful protector.

Paul understood as few of us do how totally dependent Christians are upon the grace of the Lord Jesus Christ. He saw that we need the merits of his death for our pardon, the power of his life for our service, and the protection of his presence for our endurance. The more we appreciate our reliance upon him, the more we will love him and live for him.

Christian Obedience

⁴We have confidence in the Lord that you are doing and will continue to do the things we command. ⁵May the Lord direct your hearts into God's love and Christ's perseverance.

⁶In the name of the Lord Jesus Christ, we command you, brothers, to keep away from every brother who is idle and does not live according to the teaching you received from us. ⁷For you yourselves know how you ought to follow our example. We were not idle when we were with you, ⁸nor did we eat anyone's food without paying for it. On the contrary, we worked night and day, labouring and toiling so that we would not be a burden to any of you. ⁹We did this, not because we do not have the right to such help, but in order to make ourselves a model for you to follow. ¹⁰For even when we were with you, we gave you this rule: 'If a man will not work, he shall not eat' (2 Thess. 3:4–10).

Paul's request for prayer (vv.1–3) glides almost imperceptibly into instruction on church discipline. Burdened though he is to see the gospel spread rapidly, he is also dedicated to seeing his converts living obediently. And ongoing problems in Thessalonica called for immediate corrective action.

These problems, as becomes plain in the lengthy section that completes this letter, related to a disorderly minority of church members who were refusing to work. We have already been introduced to this group in Paul's first letter and noted the special instructions he gave them there (*1 Thess.* 4:11–12). Apparently, however, they had ignored his teaching, and the problems connected with them had worsened. Sterner measures were needed if they were to be brought into line, measures that are outlined in directions given to the loyal majority in the congregation in the verses before us.

CONFIDENCE

In keeping with his great tact, the apostle approaches this subject indirectly. In the opening words of this final chapter he has asked for their prayers (vv.1–2) and assured them that their faithful Lord would protect them from the evil one (v.3). This leads him to express his confidence in their present and future obedience (v.4) and to pray for the Lord's grace in their hearts (v.5). Only then does he issue commands on how to deal with the rebellious faction in the church (v.6).

Aware as he is that there are some who are defying his instructions, the apostle is nevertheless confident that the church as a whole is doing what he has commanded (v.4). The problem he must address involves recalcitrant individuals, not the whole congregation, and he wants to assure the faithful of his confidence in them.

His confidence rested in them not as people, but in the Lord. He knew that left to themselves they were all liable to rebellion, as indeed we all are. But he had abundant evidence that the Lord Jesus was powerfully at work in them, and that through his grace they were not only presently obeying his commands but would continue to do so.

This reliance upon the Lord prompts another fervent prayer wish from the apostle. Their continued obedience depends upon the state of their hearts, the inner source of life that controls words and actions. He wants their hearts to be filled with God's own love and Christ's perseverance (v.5) and prays that the Lord would remove any obstacles to that being the case. Strengthened with that love and perseverance they will be able to do all that is required of them.

Ultimately, our ability to do the Lord's will does not depend on our own resources. While we are bound to do what God says, it is only as we live in the Lord, relying on his grace and seeking his enabling, that we can acceptably perform the least of his requirements.

COMMAND

From commendation, Paul now moves to command. He is ready to take up the problem of idle and disruptive church members and introduces what he has to say about them in a distinctly military tone (v.6). There can be no mistaking the nature of what he is about to say. He is emphatically commanding the Thessalonian Christians to follow a course of action. And he is doing this not on his own account, but in the name of the Lord Jesus. His words come with all the authority of the Lord himself and are in perfect accord with his will.

The action he wants the congregation to take is toward those who are idle and are not following the teachings of the apostle and his missionary helpers (v.6). We need to note that the objects of this action are considered to be 'brothers'. They are not unbelievers who have wormed their way into the congregation, nor are they to be regarded as people who have been excommunicated (*1 Cor.* 5:9–13). Fellow believers are in view, but believers who are nevertheless living in a disorderly way. They have broken rank with the rest of the congregation by refusing to accept and live according to the body of teaching that had been passed on to them by the missionaries. Their fault is not one of unbelief but of disobedience.

The congregation is to keep away from all who belong to this category. By this Paul means they are to withdraw from intimate fellowship with such people. They are not to regard them as outcasts, but they are not to associate with them, either. They cannot let themselves be drawn into their pattern of life, nor can they act in a way that seems to approve of what they are doing. They must hold themselves aloof from them to make their disapproval clear.

Discipline by separation is never easy, and is certainly not something widely practised in western churches today. Where it is, it is often ridiculed as arrogance. But Paul is in no way hinting that the loyal members in the congregation are in any sense superior. He wants them to keep free from fault and put corrective pressure on those who are erring. Discipline never aims to destroy, but to restore.

EXAMPLE

Paul's readers really did not need any more teaching on this subject of idleness. Not only had they received plenty already (v.10), but they had been shown how to live by the apostle and his associates while they were with them. Paul, Silas and Timothy had been both messengers of the gospel and models of how Christians were to live. The

Thessalonians had understood from the outset that they were meant to follow their example (v.7, *1 Thess.* 1:6), even as the missionaries were following the example of the Lord Jesus himself (*1 Cor.* 11:1). And their example had not been one of idleness.

On the contrary, they had worked night and day to avoid being burdensome (v.8). Though entitled to material support as ambassadors of the Lord Jesus (v.9), the three men had foregone this right in the interests of the gospel. They made a policy of refusing to eat anyone's food without paying for it (v.7). Even when staying with Jason, one of the early believers in the city (*Acts* 17:5–9), Paul chose to work with his hands rather than to be a burden to his host.

But not being a burden was only part of the reason for working (*1 Thess.* 2:9). In part, too, it was to provide a model for new believers to follow (v.9). Cities in the ancient world were littered with beggars and mendicants of various kinds. Paul did not want new believers adopting a dependent or lazy lifestyle, but wanted them to work quietly and productively with their own hands (*1 Thess.* 4:11–12). Not content simply to tell them this – something that he obviously did repeatedly (v.10) – the apostle set out to show them by his own actions how it was to be done. If the Christians in Thessalonica were to take the time to recall, they would understand that they could not allow anyone among them to be idle and disruptive.

Paul's personal example, then, adds weight to his demand that the church withdraw from those who were being disobedient. While his word as the representative of the Lord Jesus (v.6) was sufficient, his personal example made that word the more credible and compelling.

All in positions of authority will find their directives more readily received if they can say, 'Do not just listen to what I say, but imitate what I do.'

12

Dealing with the Disorderly

11We hear that some among you are idle. They are not busy; they are busybodies. 12Such people we command and urge in the Lord Jesus Christ to settle down and earn the bread they eat. 13And as for you, brothers, never tire of doing what is right.

14If anyone does not obey our instruction in this letter, take special note of him. Do not associate with him, in order that he may feel ashamed. 15Yet do not regard him as an enemy, but warn him as a brother (2 Thess. 3:11–15).

The congregation in Thessalonica had to do something about its idle members. These people were living out of step with the pattern Paul and his helpers had taught and demonstrated while with them (vv.7–10). They were not only endangering the reputation of the gospel, but they were also making themselves a burden to the congregation. And perhaps even worse, they were actually rebelling against the clear teaching of the apostles.

Paul has already told the congregation what it has to do with these unruly members (v.6). In this section he addresses the offenders themselves, then adds fuller directions to guide the faithful brothers in their dealings with any who should not heed his loving but firm demands.

THE OFFENDERS

The apostle knew that he was on firm ground in making so much of this issue. News had reached him – though he did not let on the source of his information – that idle members were indeed troubling the congregation (v.11). The offenders appear to be only a minority group in the church, but they are a troublesome group just the same.

They are described as idle because they apparently were unwilling to work to provide for their daily needs. This may have been because they disliked manual labour, or they thought that physical work was inconsistent with living in heavenly places with Christ (*Eph*. 2:6). But more likely, they were not working because they thought that Jesus' return was so near at hand that it was not only unnecessary but wrong to be immersed in such mundane concerns as earning money to put food on one's plate. Whatever the cause, they were not actively engaged in working for their keep.

This did not mean that they were totally inactive. In a neat play on words the apostle describes them as 'not busy', but 'busybodies' (v.11). With time on their hands, they occupied themselves meddling in other people's affairs (*1 Tim*. 5:13). The term suggests that they would not leave other people alone. Not content with keeping their convictions to themselves, they pestered and interrupted other people. They may well have considered themselves the more spiritual members of the church and seen it their duty to reproach others for their lack of zeal. While happy to live off the charity of their diligent brothers and sisters, they did their best to keep the very hands that fed them from working. Such people are always troublesome nuisances in churches.

THEIR CORRECTION

Turning now to these people, the apostle addresses them directly yet impersonally. He reveals his tact by not accosting them bluntly in words like, 'Listen now, you idlers!' Instead, he writes, 'Such people . . .' (v.12). It is as though he were saying, 'If the cap fits, wear it.' Nobody could claim they had been humiliated, but equally, none could escape what he was saying. The guilty would know they were being spoken to.

They are addressed both authoritatively and persuasively. Paul commands them as one relaying instructions from a superior. He wants his words not only to be heard but also to be obeyed. At the same time he speaks with passionate earnestness, urging them to heed his instructions.

Then, too, his appeal is made on the basis of their being in the Lord Jesus together. As believers in the Lord they have become new people in a new situation. Because they are now in the Lord Jesus Christ, they must live in ways that are in keeping with their new position. This, more than any simple claim to authority, provides a powerful motive for their obedience.

What does the apostle want them to do? They are to settle down and earn their bread (v.12). They are to stop their disruptive interfering in the lives of other people and take care of their own affairs. If they have become overexcited about the second coming of Jesus, they are to calm down. And especially, as Paul had written earlier, they are to get their hands busy at some productive work and earn enough to feed themselves and meet their other daily needs (*1 Thess.* 4:11–12).

Straight talking of this sort is needed at times in the life of the church. Usually Christian behaviour can be guided by teaching principles of conduct and outlining general pathways for practice. Where people are stumbling, gentle admonitions may also be needed. But stubborn rebellion, such as was the case in Thessalonica, calls for strong correction in the plainest of words. Failure to deal as boldly with disorder as Paul did in this case lies behind many of the problems crippling churches today.

THE PATIENT MAJORITY

Most of Paul's readers did not need these stiff words of correction. He had something else to say to this larger group. They did not need correction so much as encouragement. 'As for you brothers', he adds endearingly, identifying himself closely with them in the Lord, over against the smaller group he has been addressing, 'never tire of doing what is right' (v.13).

In contrast to the idlers, the majority were doing what was right, quietly working to supply their needs and minding their own affairs. As difficult as that might be at times, especially in the face of the enthusiastic arguments and slovenly behaviour of the non-workers in the congregation, they were to keep at it without flagging. They were not to let those who were failing in their duty hinder them from doing theirs. They must not grow weary in well doing (*Gal.* 6:9).

We must not let the wayward behaviour of other Christians discourage us from doing what we know to be right. Even when their failure makes life more difficult for us, we must continue to show forbearance and faithfulness. Delinquency on their part is no excuse for unfaithfulness on ours.

STERNER MEASURES

That is not to say, however, that we should endlessly accommodate those who are disobedient. Persistent rebellion calls for sterner measures than words. Paul recognised that there might well be need for such sterner measures in Thessalonica, and therefore outlines the actions the church must take should there be anyone who does not obey these instructions (v.14). In the case of such a person, the church is required to do three things.

It must first take special note of them (v.14). Paul does not say how this is to be done. Some suggest he wants the offender to be cited or named in one of the public meetings of the church. While this may be the case, he may also have something less severe in mind. He may simply want people to make a mental note of the person concerned. Whatever is in view, the apostle intends something more than cursory recognition. He wants offenders to be noted as offenders and marked as people that must be dealt with in a definite way. They cannot be overlooked.

Secondly, the church must not associate with such a person, so that he might feel ashamed (v.16). Here the apostle repeats and elaborates his earlier command (v.6). This non-association order is again a call to withdrawal from intimate fellowship. Paul is not telling the church to exclude such a person from their congregation altogether, as he later tells the Corinthians in the case of the man guilty of gross sexual sin (*1 Cor.* 5:5). The action contemplated is not excommunication, but correction brought about by social ostracism. Church members are not to welcome such a person into the intimacies of home and church fellowship as they might have done in the past. When words fail, they are to exert pressure upon them by withdrawing personal intimacy.

Through exclusion from close personal fellowship, the erring brother is to be made to think deeply about what he is doing. When that happens, he will perhaps come to his senses, repent of his sin, and enjoy the restoration of relationships within the church.

Finally, the church is to go about this act of discipline in the right spirit. They are not to treat the erring person as an enemy, but warn him as a brother (v.15). There is no place for harshness or hostility when trying to correct fellow Christians. No matter how repugnant their sin, they are not to be treated as our personal enemies. Our task is to admonish and warn them as fellow members of Christ. The point may be reached where we can no longer regard them in this way and must exclude them from the church, but until that time we must aim at their reformation and not their humiliation.

13

Final Words

16Now may the Lord of peace himself give you peace at all times and in every way. The Lord be with all of you.

17I, Paul, write this greeting in my own hand, which is the distinguishing mark in all my letters. This is how I write.

18The grace of our Lord Jesus Christ be with all of you (2 Thess. 3:16–18).

Paul has completed his task. He has encouraged his suffering readers, corrected their wrong ideas about the day of the Lord, and given instructions to and about idlers in the congregation. His pastoral obligations have been fulfilled, at least for the moment, and his heart concerns put to rest.

All that remains for him to do is to say farewell. Yet for the apostle, even this is no perfunctory formality. To the very end, his words are loaded with meaning appropriate to the circumstances of his readers. We cannot afford to hurry over a single one of them.

A PRAYER FOR PEACE

The prayer of verse 16 signals the approaching end of the letter, but it also flows out of the instructions that precede it. Paul has been urging the congregation to deal firmly with persistent idlers and has spoken directly to these offenders themselves. He wants the disruption they are causing to be brought to a speedy end. But in this case, as always, he knows that unaided human effort cannot rectify spiritual problems. Unless the Lord Jesus strengthens the readers, his words will be wasted.

Consistent with this, he prays that the Lord would give them peace (v.16). He recognises that peace, in the broad sense of spiritual health and wholeness, is what the congregation needs. If they have the peace with God that comes through the cross of Christ, and enjoy the grace of God that flows from being in fellowship with him, their disorders will be put right and their strained relationships restored. True wholeness will be restored to the church as the anxious are calmed, the frustrated settled, and the unruly made compliant.

The source of this peace is the Lord of peace himself, the Lord Jesus Christ. Men cannot manufacture it, for it is nothing less than the peace that fills the Lord himself. The fact that elsewhere God is spoken of as the God of peace (*Rom.* 15:33, *1 Thess.* 5:23) is a further token of how closely the Father and Son are related in giving life to the church. The church is truly both in God the Father and in the Lord Jesus Christ (1:1). Both form the single reservoir of its spiritual resources.

Paul prays that his readers would experience that peace abundantly. He asks the Lord to give it to them at all times and in every way (v.16). He wants the peace of the Lord Jesus to be their unbroken possession in every circumstance that confronts them. The grace of the Lord Jesus is not something we need only on special occasions. We need it to sustain us every moment of each day. For that reason, the Christian life must be one of constant leaning upon the Lord through prayer for strength.

Indeed, Paul sums up his desire for the Thessalonians in the prayer, 'The Lord be with all of you' (v.16). The Lord's peace and all his other blessings come through his presence. They do not exist independently in themselves. They exist only in him and are conveyed to us as he lives in us through his Spirit. To pray that the Lord would be with us is to pray that we would be filled with every spiritual blessing through him.

Paul wants this for all of his readers, including those who are disobedient and causing problems in the church. That they are causing their fellow believers irritation and him extra burden does not lessen his genuine desire for their well-being. Quite the opposite is the case. He knows that the disorderly members of the congregation, more than others, need the calming effect of the Lord's peace and presence.

His generous fellow-feeling toward troublemakers in the church is a lesson to us. We often want to see them punished in some way, or at least deprived of spiritual blessing. Paul shames such mean thoughts by showing us that these people, as well as ourselves, need the grace that flows from the Lord's presence.

A SIGNATURE GREETING

With that all-encompassing prayer, Paul now feels at liberty to bring his letter to an end. He does so, in keeping with the pattern of his day, with a final word of greeting or farewell. In other letters, he passes on greetings from friends and associates and asks his readers to greet others in turn (*Rom.* 16:16, *2 Cor.* 13:12, *Col.* 4:10–15.). But here a personal word of greeting suffices.

In this instance the apostle draws attention to the fact that he is writing it with his own hand (v.17). Letter writers in his day commonly dictated their letters to a professional scribe and added the final greeting in their own writing as the equivalent of our personal signature. Paul apparently did this in all his letters, although he does not always make reference to the fact (*Col.* 4:18, *Gal.* 6:11; cf. *Eph.* 6:21).

That he should mention it here and add the explanation that it is a distinguishing mark in all his letters, was probably on account of the circumstances of his readers. Paul knew that the rebellious faction in the congregation might want to dispute the genuineness of the letter when it was read to them. He had written critically of them, spoken sharply to them, and given firm directions regarding them. They might well try to protect themselves by claiming that the letter was not from Paul and did not have apostolic authority. These final words in his handwriting would silence them. They were indisputable proof of the genuineness of the letter.

Furthermore, forged letters supposedly from Paul had already troubled the congregation (2:2). The apostle did not want that to happen again and provides a way in which his readers can recognise letters that do come from him. All bear the distinctive seal of his own handwritten final greetings. Apparently his readers know what his writing looks like, for he adds, 'This is how I write' (v.17). Whenever they see that script on a letter, they can be sure it is from him.

A FINAL BLESSING

In words almost identical to those with which he ended his first letter (*1 Thess.* 5:28), the apostle bids farewell to his readers with the blessing, 'The grace of our Lord Jesus Christ be with all of you' (v.18).

Again, it needs to be stressed that these last words are no empty formality. Common as it may be for Paul to end his letters with them, or with words like them (*1 Cor.* 16:23, *Gal.* 6:18, *Phil.* 4:23), they yet express a genuine wish for his readers. He knows that the supreme need of all Christians is the grace of the Lord Jesus Christ. The same free love of God in Christ that first calls us to him is needed throughout life to sustain and perfect us in him (*Phil.* 1:5). Paul acknowledges this at the beginning of this letter (1:2) and ends it on the same note.

Given the pressures from a hostile world, as well as the troubles bubbling within the church, these words must have breathed comfort into the hearts of the Thessalonians. The promised grace of their all-powerful and all-loving Lord and Saviour offered hope in their difficult circumstances. In him they could find all that they needed to continue their work, their labour, and their patient endurance as they waited for his coming.

It hardly needs to be said that this same grace of our Lord Jesus Christ remains the indispensable need for us, too. We can face whatever the future holds for us with confidence knowing that the limitless resources of our Lord Jesus are at our disposal. James Edmeston put it well when he wrote:

> Fountain of grace rich, full and free,
> What need I that is not in thee,
> For pardon, strength to meet the day,
> And peace which none can take away.

Group Study Guide

SCHEME FOR GROUP BIBLE STUDY
(Covering 13 Weeks)

	Study Passage	Chapters
1.	1 Thessalonians 1:1–10	1–4
2.	1 Thessalonians 2:1–16	5–9
3.	1 Thessalonians 2:17–3:5	10–11
4.	1 Thessalonians 3:6–13	12–13
5.	1 Thessalonians 4:1–12	14–17
6.	1 Thessalonians 4:13–18	18–19
7.	1 Thessalonians 5:1–11	20–22
8.	1 Thessalonians 5:12–28	23–26
9.	2 Thessalonians 1:1–12	1–5
10.	2 Thessalonians 2:1–8	6–7
11.	2 Thessalonians 2:9–17	8–9
12.	2 Thessalonians 3:1–10	10–11
13.	2 Thessalonians 3:11–18	12–13

This Study Guide has been prepared for group Bible study, but it can also be used individually. Those who use it on their own may find it helpful to keep a notebook of their responses.

The way in which group Bible studies are led can greatly enhance their value. A well-conducted study will appear as though it has been easy to lead, but that is usually because the leader has worked hard and planned well. Clear aims are essential.

AIMS

In all Bible study, individual or corporate, we have several aims:

1. To gain an understanding of the original meaning of the particular passage of Scripture;

2. To apply this to ourselves and our own situation;

3. To develop some specific ways of putting the biblical teaching into practice.

2 Timothy 3:16–17 provides a helpful structure. Paul says that Scripture is useful for:

(i) teaching us;

(ii) rebuking us;

(iii) correcting, or changing us;

(iv) training us in righteousness.

Consequently, in studying any passage of Scripture, we should always have in mind these questions:

What does this passage teach us (about God, ourselves, etc.)?

Does it rebuke us in some way?

How can its teaching transform us?

What equipment does it give us for serving Christ?

In fact, these four questions alone would provide a safe guide in any Bible study.

PRINCIPLES

In group Bible study we meet in order to learn about God's Word and ways 'together with all the saints' *(Eph.* 3:18). But our own experience, as well as Scripture, tells us that the saints are not always what they *are* called to be in every situation – including group Bible study! Leaders ordinarily have to work hard and prepare well if the work of the group is to be spiritually profitable. The following guidelines for leaders may help to make this a reality.

Preparation:

1. Study and understand the passage yourself. The better prepared and more sure of the direction of the study you are, the more likely it is that the group will have a beneficial and enjoyable study.

Ask: What are the main things this passage is saying? How can this be made clear? This is not the same question as the more common 'What does this passage "say to you"?' which expects a reaction rather than an exposition of the passage. Be clear about that distinction yourself, and work at making it clear in the group study.

2. On the basis of your own study form a clear idea *before* the group meets of (i) the main theme(s) of the passage which should be opened out for discussion, and (ii) some general conclusions the group ought to reach as a result of the study. Here the questions which arise from 2 Timothy 3:16–17 should act as our guide.

3. The guidelines and questions which follow may help to provide a general framework for each discussion; leaders should use them as starting places which can be further developed. It is usually helpful to have a specific goal or theme in mind for group discussion, and one is suggested for each study. But even more important than tracing a single theme is understanding the teaching and the implications of the passage.

Leading the Group:

1. Announce the passage and theme for the study, and begin with prayer. In group studies it may be helpful to invite a different person to lead in prayer each time you meet.

2. Introduce the passage and theme, briefly reminding people of its outline and highlighting the content of each subsidiary section.

3. Lead the group through the discussion questions. Use your own if you are comfortable in doing so; those provided may be used, developing them with your own points. As discussion proceeds, continue to encourage the group first of all to discuss the significance of the passage (teaching) and only then its application (meaning for us). It may be helpful to write important points and applications on a board by way of summary as well as visual aid.

4. At the end of each meeting, remind members of the group of their assignments for the next meeting, and encourage them to come prepared. Be sufficiently prepared as the leader to give specific assignments to individuals, or even couples or groups, to come with specific contributions ('John, would you try to find out something about the 'man of lawlessness' for the next meeting?' 'Fiona, would you see what you can find out about the different ways in which 1 Thessalonians 5:14–17 has been interpreted?').

5. Remember that you are the leader of the group! Encourage clear contributions, and do not be embarrassed to ask someone to explain what they have said more fully or to help them to do so ('Do you mean . . . ?').

Most groups include the 'over-talkative', the 'over-silent' and the 'red-herring raisers'! Leaders must control the first, encourage the second and redirect the third! Each leader will develop his or her own most natural way of doing that; but it will be helpful to think out what that is before the occasion arises! The first two groups can be helped by some judicious direction of questions to specific individuals or even groups (*e.g.*, 'How do those who are not working outside of the home apply this?' 'Jane, you know something about this from personal experience . . .'); the third by redirecting the discussion to the passage itself ('That is an interesting point, but isn't it true that this passage really concentrates on . . . ?'). It may be helpful to break the group up into smaller groups sometimes, giving each subgroup specific points to discuss and to report back on. A wise arranging of these smaller groups may also help each member to participate.

More important than any techniques we may develop is the help of the Spirit enabling us to understand and to apply the Scriptures. Have and encourage a humble, prayerful spirit.

6. Keep faith with the schedule; it is better that some of the group wished the study could have been longer than that others are inconvenienced by it stretching beyond the time limits set.

7. Close in prayer. As time permits, spend the closing minutes in corporate prayer, encouraging the group to apply what they have learned in praise and thanks, intercession and petition.

STUDY 1: 1 Thessalonians1: 1-10

AIM: To identify the characteristics of a living New Testament church.

1. Acts 17:1–9 tells us how the Thessalonian church came into being. What was central to its birth (vv.3–4)? Does this have anything to teach us about (i) the message, and (ii) the manner of evangelism and mission work today?

2. The community of people that believed the gospel is described as being 'in God the Father and the Lord Jesus Christ' (v.1). What does Paul mean by this? If it is true of us today as well, how should it affect the way we live?

3. The church at Thessalonica was notable for its 'work . . . labour . . . and endurance' (v.3), qualities that always mark healthy, spiritual churches. What is the source of these qualities, and how can church leaders promote them?

4. The Holy Spirit was vitally active in bringing the Thessalonian church into being (v.5) and in supporting young believers in the fires of opposition (v.6). In what specific ways did he do this? Can we expect him to work in these same ways in our churches today?

5. Why is it so inevitable that people meet with opposition (v.6) when they become Christians?

6. The gospel revolutionised the lives of those in Thessalonica who received it (vv.9–10). What changes did it produce? Should we look for similar responses when people become Christians today?

7. Changed lives are noticed and witness to the reality of the gospel. Can churches fail to impact the world because they have become too much like the world? In what ways are we tempted to conform to the world? How can we resist?

FOR STUDY 2: Read 1 Thessalonians 2:1–16 and chapters 5–9.

STUDY 2: 1 Thessalonians 2:1–16

AIM: To consider the nature of genuine Christian ministry and learn from this how we can serve God more effectively.

1. One mark of a genuine ministry is willingness to press on in spite of opposition and difficulties. How did this show itself in the ministry of Paul, Silas and Timothy in Thessalonica (v.2)? What approach would people driven by self-seeking motives be likely to take in this situation?

2. What was it that drove the missionaries to carry on preaching the gospel (v.4)? Can this be an incentive for our ministries today as well, or was it something unique to apostolic times?

3. Motives and methods are often closely linked. Self-seeking opportunists are likely to use any means that will get them what they want. How did Paul's motives affect his methods (see also *1 Cor.* 2:1–5, *2 Cor.* 2:17; 4:1–2)? Can a passion for 'results' lead to pragmatic and sinful approaches in Christian ministry today?

4. Paul was ready to forego his rights and put himself to no little trouble to make sure that he did not put a stumbling block in the way of any who were interested in the gospel (vv.6b–9). Are we in danger of letting a worldly 'user pays' attitude rob us of this spirit in our church and evangelistic ministries today?

5. How did Paul's manner of dealing with young converts in Thessalonica (vv.7–8) differ from the tactics of self-appointed apostles in the Corinthian church (*2 Cor.* 11:20)? Some might regard his approach as too soft. Why is it the only way, however, that is consistent with the gospel?

6. What goal did Paul have in view as he encouraged, comforted and urged the young Thessalonian converts (v.12)? Is this approach to discipling different from putting new believers through structured discipling programmes?

7. Paul saw himself as a transmitter of God's word, the gospel, and believed that God worked through that word to change lives (v.13). How does God's word work to bring about change in people? What does this say about the place we should give to teaching and preaching the Bible in witness and ministry today?

8. Opposition is a mark of a genuine ministry. In what ways are we likely to face opposition as we let God's word shape our attitudes and actions with regard to (a) marriage, (b) entertainment, and (c) education?

FOR STUDY 3: Read 1 Thessalonians 2:17–3:5 and chapters 10–11.

STUDY 3: 1 Thessalonians 2:17–3:5

AIM: To recognise features of true spiritual care in order to become more caring members of the Christian community.

1. Physical separation from the Thessalonians did not stop Paul and his companions caring deeply for them (v.17). Out of sight, they were not out of mind. Why do we tend to lose concern for people when we become separated from them, and how can we overcome this?

2. Paul's care for his converts did not stop at earnest feelings and sympathetic words. How did it express itself in practical ways? Is there a danger of being content with kind thoughts and nice words when we should do more to help those in need (see *1 John* 3:16–18)? If so, what should we do to overcome this?

3. Is it wrong to serve others with a view to the joy we will know when Jesus returns? Is not this a form of self-seeking?

4. How important is team effort in effective ministry? Can individualism, or the desire to do everything by ourselves, rob us of ways of serving others?

5. Paul was more concerned about the faith of his converts than their physical needs or comforts. Is there a tendency to be more concerned about the temporal rather than spiritual needs of people within the church today?

6. Paul sent Timothy both to 'find out' about the faith of the Thessalonian Christians (3:5), and to 'strengthen and encourage' them in it (3:2). How can we go about 'strengthening' and 'encouraging' others in their faith?

7. There is a common saying that 'forewarned is fore-armed'. Paul and his missionary helpers had repeatedly warned their converts in Thessalonica to expect suffering (3:3–4). Should we make a point of warning young Christians about the trials they will face from the world, the flesh and the devil? Do we tend to downplay this out of fear that it will be off-putting?

8. Paul was aware that Satan was opposing his efforts to return to Thessalonica (2:18) and tempting new believers there to turn from their faith (3:5). How should our belief in the opposition of a personal devil affect our Christians service?

FOR STUDY 4: Read 1 Thessalonians 3:6–13 and chapters 12–13.

STUDY 4: 1 Thessalonians 3:6–13

AIM: To consider some of the encouragements we can know in Christian ministry.

1. Timothy's report after visiting Thessalonica refreshed and encouraged Paul. What three pieces of news seem to have especially encouraged him (v.6)? Why did they have this effect on him?

2. How important is good communication to keeping relationships alive and productive? What can happen when communication either is delayed or breaks down?

3. The good news of the Thessalonians' steadfast faith breathed new life into Paul and his co-workers (v.8). Words of encouragement can be a great spur to preserving effort in difficult ministries. Do we pay enough attention to encouraging one another? How can we do this sincerely without falling into the trap of simply flattering each other?

4. How does spiritual joy (v.9) differ from mere happiness? Can it co-exist with suffering and even sadness (see 1:6 and *2 Cor.* 6:10)?

5. What impact did Timothy's report have on the prayer life of the missionary team (v.10)? Does this offer a clue as to what it takes to keep up fervent intercession for others? What do we need to do if we want people to pray for us?

6. Paul, Silas and Timothy prayed that God would remove the obstacles that hindered them from visiting the Thessalonians (v.11). Do we view prayer as a practical force in Christian ministry? Do we give it sufficient priority in the life and witness of our churches?

7. Can we live more holy and loving lives simply by trying to do so (vv.12–13)? What else besides our own efforts is needed, and how can we obtain it?

8. Does the approaching return of the Lord Jesus affect the way we live today, or is it little more than a theoretical possibility lying somewhere in the distant future? How can we rectify this if it is a problem?

FOR STUDY 5: Read 1 Thessalonians 4:1–12 and chapters 14–17.

STUDY 5: 1 Thessalonians 4:1–12

AIM: To consider what it means to live a life pleasing to God.

1. Is the Christian life a matter of abiding by rules, or fulfilling the demands of a relationship? Or does it involve both?

2. 'Obedience is never a supplement to God's grace, but it is always the fitting response to it' (p.63). What are some of the ways we can fall into the trap of trying to earn God's favour by our efforts?

3. Why is it important to press on towards perfection in the Christian life (vv.1, 10), even if we can never attain it in our present state? Do we settle too easily for mediocrity in Christian living today?

4. Human sinfulness finds expression especially in the realm of sexual promiscuity and perversion (*Rom.* 1:24–27). Why do these particular sins seem to be so predominant in unregenerate man? What do the so-called 'liberated' views of sex in modern cultures say about their spiritual state?

5. How would you describe a healthy biblical code for sexual conduct?

6. Is the fear of a future judgement a reason for living a holy life (v.6), or is this inconsistent with experiencing God's grace in Christ?

7. What are some of the hindrances preventing 'a warm spirit of Christian kinship among all true believers' (p.72) today?

8. Intense interest in spiritual affairs is often accompanied by irresponsibility in everyday living. What lies at the root of this problem, and how can it be overcome?

FOR STUDY 6: Read 1 Thessalonians 4:13–18 and chapters 18–19.

STUDY 6: 1 Thessalonians 4:13–18

AIM: To understand better what will happen to Christians when Jesus comes back again.

1. What specific concern is Paul addressing in this section of his letter? Is he giving a comprehensive, general outline of events that will occur at the second coming of Jesus, or does he have a more focused pastoral purpose in view (see vv. 13, 15, 18)? Is this important to keep in mind when interpreting this passage?

2. What does it mean to 'sleep in Jesus' (vv. 13–14)? Is Paul teaching the doctrine of 'soul sleep' here, the idea that the dead remain in a state of unconsciousness until the second coming of Christ?

3. Is it wrong for Christians to grieve when they suffer bereavement? If not, how should their sorrow differ from that of the world (v. 13)?

4. How does the historical fact that Jesus died and rose again prove that Christians who have died will return with him when he comes again?

5. According to this section, what sequence of events will take place at the *parousia* ('presence' or 'coming') of Jesus?

6. Many Christians are hesitant to talk about the 'rapture' because it has come to be associated with a particular interpretation of events that will occur at the end of the age. What does the term refer to, and is it valid to use it in reference to events at the *parousia*?

7. Paul views being ever present with the Lord at his return (v. 17) as the goal or climax of salvation. Is this the way we commonly view salvation, or do we tend to think of it more in terms of dying and going to be with Jesus in heaven?

8. In what sense is it true to say that 'Christian comfort is grounded in more than sympathy' (p. 85)? What does this require of us if we are to provide solid comfort for others?

FOR STUDY 7: Read 1 Thessalonians 5:1–11 and chapters 20–22.

STUDY 7: 1 Thessalonians 5:1–11

AIM: To learn more of how the second coming of Christ will affect people when it takes place.

1. The history of the Christian church has been littered with people obsessed with sign-seeking and predicting the time of the Lord's return. Why are these activities mistaken and unhelpful as a way of preparing for the Lord's return (vv.1–2)?

2. Why is the return of the Lord Jesus referred to as 'the day of the Lord' (v.2)? Does this term have any special significance?

3. Why does the certainty of the coming of the Lord need to be 'heralded urgently and clearly' (p.88) in our generation?

4. Is the 'destruction' in store for the unsuspecting mass of mankind (v.3) the same as annihilation?

5. Why will Christians not be surprised in the same way as others (v.4) by the return of the Lord?

6. If trying to pinpoint the precise time of the Lord's return is not the best way to get ready for his coming, what is?

7. As awesome and frightening as the day of the Lord will be, Christians need not tremble as they think of it. What is it that takes away the fear of that day (vv.9–10)?

8. Do the ministries of comfort and encouragement belong exclusively to the trained leadership of the church, or are they the common task of all Christians? In what ways can the ministries be exercised?

FOR STUDY 8: Read 1 Thessalonians 5:12–28 and chapters 23–26.

STUDY 8: 1 Thessalonians 5:12–28

AIM: To understand how the gospel should affect church life.

1. Leaders are often the butt of criticism in churches, just as they are in society at large. How should Christians view their leaders, and why is it so important that they do regard them in this way?

2. Churches will invariably contain 'problem children', those whose personal characteristics and spiritual maturity create special needs. How do we typically respond to such people? How, according to Paul, should they be treated (vv.14–15)?

3. Is it unrealistic of Paul to expect Christians to be joyful, prayerful and thankful at all times and in all situations (vv.16–18)? Do not our personal circumstances and daily occupations mean that we will often be too distracted and discomforted to be in this state?

4. How can we, in both our individual and congregational lives, 'put out the Spirit's fire' (v.19)?

5. Prophecy was a way in which the Holy Spirit 'nourished the life of the early church' (p.104). How were people to treat individual prophecies (vv.20–22)? Does this have any relevance to regular ministries in the church today?

6. Discuss cases where 'bizarre claims are in danger of fostering contempt for the Spirit and his gifts today just as they did in the first century' (p.105). What is the best response?

7. If sanctification is God's work (v.23), does this mean there is nothing we have to do in the process?

8. If it is true that 'too little attention is given to the practice of Christian greeting today' (p.113), what needs to be done to rectify this deficiency?

FOR STUDY 9: Read 2 Thessalonians 1:1–12 and chapters 27–31.

STUDY 9: 2 Thessalonians 1:1–12

AIM: To see how God's justice will be vindicated when the Lord Jesus returns.

1. What circumstances apparently prompted this second letter to the church in Thessalonica?

2. Was Paul in danger of flattering his readers when he spoke of 'boasting' about them to other churches (v.4), or is this a legitimate way of encouraging others? If so, does it happen as often as it should among Christians today?

3. On the surface, it does not seem just that God should let his people suffer dreadfully at the hands of those who are ungodly (vv.5–6). Why is this view of Christian suffering inadequate?

4. The idea that God will one day 'pay back' people for the wrong they have done (v.6) is not popular among many today. Why do people shy away from this notion, and why is their reaction wrong?

5. Is the revelation of Jesus from heaven 'in blazing fire with his powerful angels' (v.7) necessarily a totally separate event from the *parousia* described in 1 Thessalonians 4:13–18?

6. How will Jesus punish unbelievers and persecutors (vv.8–9) when he is revealed from heaven?

7. What will God's faithful people experience at this payback time for the ungodly (v.10)?

8. Does the promise of safety and glory when the Lord appears mean that Christians can relax and let that day come when and how it will? If not, what should their approach to it be?

FOR STUDY 10: Read 2 Thessalonians 2:1–8 and chapters 32–33.

STUDY 10: 2 Thessalonians 2:1–8

AIM: To learn more about what must happen before the Lord Jesus returns.

1. What circumstances and concerns lie behind this section (2:1–16) of Paul's letter?

2. Is the idea that certain events must occur before the coming of Jesus inconsistent with the fact that 'no one knows about that day or hour' (*Matt.* 24:36)?

3. What does the 'rebellion' mentioned in verse 3 apparently refer to?

4. What makes the term 'man of lawlessness' (v.3) a fitting description of the coming arch-agent of the devil?

5. 'Few characters of the Bible excite more curiosity than the man of lawlessness' (p.144). What features of this figure and his future activities are clear from verse 4?

6. Are the coming of future rebellion and the man of lawlessness things reserved wholly for some future time, or is there a sense in which forces preparing for these events are already active in the world? If so, what might these forces be?

7. What might Paul have had in mind when he spoke of something restraining the development of lawlessness at the present time (v.7)?

8. The ominous nature of these future events can be unsettling. What comfort can Christians have as they anticipate them (v.8)?

FOR STUDY 11: Read 2 Thessalonians 2:9–17 and chapters 34–35

STUDY 11: 2 Thessalonians 2:9–17

AIM: To discover how we can be sure of being saved when Jesus returns.

1. The coming 'lawless one' is Satan's 'blasphemous substitute for Jesus' at the end of the age (p.149). In what ways will he resemble Jesus, and in what ways will he differ from him (v.9)?

2. What kind of people will be 'taken in' or deceived by the coming man of lawlessness (v.9)? What does Paul's description of them tell us about the fundamental reason for unbelief?

3. The thought that God hardens people offends many Christians, yet this is the purpose he will accomplish through the man of lawlessness (v.11). How will he do this, and how can he do it without being the cause of sin?

4. Ultimately a Christian's certainty of being saved 'rests not on anything they have done, but on what God has done for them' (p.153). What great acts of God lie at the root of our assurance of being saved from coming wrath (2:13)?

5. The doctrine of election is often a subject of contention among Christians. How can it be a source of great comfort, gratitude and humility?

6. Sincere believers often struggle to know whether or not they are in fact God's elect people. How does one's response to the gospel help settle that issue (v.14)?

7. What activities should Christians focus their energies on as they wait for the coming of the Lord and the end of all things (vv.15–17)?

FOR STUDY 12: Read 2 Thessalonians 3:1–10 and chapters 36–37.

STUDY 12: 2 Thessalonians 3:1–10

AIM: To encourage people to (i) pray for the spread of the gospel and (ii) submit to the authority of the Scriptures.

1. Paul recognised that prayer as well as preaching was essential to his mission work and did not hesitate to enlist the prayer support of others (v.1). Is sufficient emphasis placed on the role of prayer in missions and evangelism in (i) your life, and (ii) your church?

2. Why is it so necessary to pray for the protection of gospel messengers? Is this commonly included in intercession for evangelists and missionaries, and if not, what does its omission indicate?

3. Is there something artificial about the way Paul commends his readers before he corrects them (vv.4–5), or is this a wise pastoral strategy?

4. The exercise of authority is a burning issue in the church today. How did Paul view and use the authority he had in the Lord Jesus Christ (v.6)? How does this relate to the exercise of authority in churches today?

5. What standard is to be used for instructing and correcting Christians in the way they live (v.6)?

6. Separation from other Christians (v.6) as a means of discipline is not something widely practised in churches today. Is it still relevant as a means of correcting those who are rebellious and disobedient? If so, why is it not used more often?

7. Paul both taught and lived the gospel while in Thessalonica (vv.7–10). How important is it for leaders to teach by example as well as by word? What effect does it have upon their ministry when they do, and when they do not?

FOR STUDY 13: Read 2 Thessalonians 3:11–18 and chapters 38–39.

STUDY 13: 2 Thessalonians 3:11–18

AIM: To learn more about church discipline and the way Paul concluded his letters.

1. A proper interest in others can deteriorate into meddling in their affairs. When does this happen, and why are 'idlers' (v.11) so prone to this fault?

2. Are there times when church leaders need to 'command and urge' (v.12) disorderly Christians, or was this something only an apostle could do?

3. What is the particular point of making people 'ashamed' through exclusion from intimate fellowship in the church (v.15)? What does this say about the goal of church discipline?

4. Discipline is often thought of as something harsh and even vindictive. What spirit or manner is to be shown in the exercise of church discipline (v.15)?

5. In what ways does the general neglect of discipline in churches today affect their life and witness?

6. Why did Paul make a point of writing a final word of greeting with his own hand (v.17)?

7. The grace (v.18) and peace (v.16) of the Lord are fundamental to the life and health of the church. How are they to be obtained and preserved?

FOR FURTHER READING

The following books are recommended for study of Paul's two letters to the Thessalonians.

W. Hendriksen: *1 and 2 Thessalonians*, New Testament Commentary, Banner of Truth Trust, Edinburgh, 1972

I.H. Marshall: *1 and 2 Thessalonians*, The New Century Bible Commentary, Eerdmans/Marshall, Morgan & Scott, 1983

L. Morris: *1 and 2 Thessalonians*, Tyndale New Testament Commentary, IVP, Leicester, 1984

J. R. W. Stott: *The Message of Thessalonians*, The Bible Speaks Today series, IVP, Leicester, 1991